Cambridge Elements

Elements in Politics and Society in East Asia
edited by
Erin Aeran Chung
Johns Hopkins University
Mary Alice Haddad
Wesleyan University
Benjamin L. Read
University of California, Santa Cruz

THE WELFARE STATE IN EAST ASIA

Joseph Wong
University of Toronto

CAMBRIDGE
UNIVERSITY PRESS

Shaftesbury Road, Cambridge CB2 8EA, United Kingdom

One Liberty Plaza, 20th Floor, New York, NY 10006, USA

477 Williamstown Road, Port Melbourne, VIC 3207, Australia

314–321, 3rd Floor, Plot 3, Splendor Forum, Jasola District Centre,
New Delhi – 110025, India

103 Penang Road, #05–06/07, Visioncrest Commercial, Singapore 238467

Cambridge University Press is part of Cambridge University Press & Assessment,
a department of the University of Cambridge.

We share the University's mission to contribute to society through the pursuit
of education, learning and research at the highest international levels of excellence.

www.cambridge.org
Information on this title: www.cambridge.org/9781009618403

DOI: 10.1017/9781108887120

First published 2025

A catalogue record for this publication is available from the British Library

ISBN 978-1-009-61840-3 Hardback
ISBN 978-1-108-81479-9 Paperback
ISSN 2632-7368 (online)
ISSN 2632-735X (print)

The Welfare State in East Asia

Elements in Politics and Society in East Asia

DOI: 10.1017/9781108887120
First published online: January 2025

Joseph Wong
University of Toronto

Author for correspondence: Joseph Wong, joe.wong@utoronto.ca

Abstract: During the postwar period, Japan, Taiwan, and South Korea emerged as industrial and democratic exemplars in the East Asia region. A less well-known story is of their equally remarkable achievements in social policy reform and the formation of welfare states. Section 1 of the Element provides an overview of welfare state deepening in Japan, Taiwan, and Korea and an account of why and how the developmental states institutionalized the social insurance model. Section 2 examines the drivers of social welfare universalization in Japan, Taiwan, and Korea, notably the importance of democratization. Section 3 focuses on emerging challenges to the East Asian welfare state and how it has adapted. Though Japan, South Korea, and Taiwan evolved their welfare states in a distinctive way historically, the current challenges they face and their responses have converged with other developed, post-industrial democracies.

Keywords: welfare state, East Asia, public policy, social policy, labor markets

ISBNs: 9781009618403 (HB), 9781108814799 (PB), 9781108887120 (OC)
ISSNs: 2632-7368 (online), 2632-735X (print)

Contents

Introduction

The East Asia region is often noted for its "miracles." Economically backward, primarily agricultural, having just emerged from decades of colonial rule in Korea and Taiwan, and in the case of Japan, rebuilding from the ashes of the Second World War, East Asian economies were among the poorest in the world in the immediate postwar period. Over the next several decades, Japan, South Korea, and Taiwan rapidly grew their economies, diversified their industries and exemplified a model of developmental statism that late developers in Asia as well as other developing countries around the world have tried to emulate (Haggard, 1990).

These were not only miracle economies, however; they also underwent tremendous political transformations in the postwar period (Slater and Wong, 2022). Supposedly culturally hardwired to be inimical to liberal democracy (Huntington, 1991; Pye, 1985), Japan in the 1950s, then followed by South Korea and Taiwan during the 1990s, became consolidated democracies. Asian values and Confucian culture did not impede their political modernization, with the end of authoritarian rule, the institutionalization of multiparty elections, the thickening of civil society, and eventual turnovers among ruling parties occurring in all three cases. That democracy has remained resilient in Japan, South Korea, and Taiwan, while in other regions democratic backsliding has become increasingly prevalent, reflects the truly miraculous political transformations that took place in the region.

Generally speaking, the democratic and economic dynamos of East Asia are credited with achieving only two miracles: economic and political. This Element contends, however, that Japan, South Korea, and Taiwan should also be considered *social welfare miracles*. The evolution and deepening of social welfare regimes in East Asia are stories that are less well-known and much less studied, yet no less significant when one considers the substantial growth and expansion of social welfare protection in Japan, South Korea, and Taiwan during the postwar period, despite the constraints faced by the region's developmental states (Peng and Wong, 2010; Peng and Wong, 2008; Ramesh, 2004; Goodman and Peng, 1996).

To be sure, the imperatives of economic growth and the geopolitical pressures of the Cold War initially frustrated efforts by progressive social policymakers and societal activists to institute sweeping social welfare reforms. Economic growth trumped economic redistribution in postwar East Asia, especially in South Korea and Taiwan. To the extent that social policies were introduced, such as in education or health, they were rationalized as investments in economic productivity (Holliday, 2000). These were poor economies, after all, for which redistributive social welfare was a luxury they could not fiscally afford, which was the case even in Japan as its economy looked to rebound after the devastation of the war. Furthermore, cultural norms about the central role of family and kinship networks posed obstacles to the introduction of government-provided social welfare. So-called "oikonomic" welfare arrangements anchored in households rather than the state were dominant in East Asian societies (Jones, 1993; Jones, 1990).

And yet, as this Element will demonstrate, social spending by the governments in Japan, South Korea, and Taiwan increased dramatically throughout the postwar period and has continued into the twenty-first century (see Table 1). Social policies and programs expanded in terms of their benefits and scope of coverage, evolving from company-based social insurance limited to few workers during the early stages of industrialization, to more universal and redistributive social protection schemes, and then to targeted programs for precarious workers, their dependents and unemployed workers.

Critics will argue, persuasively, that the East Asian welfare regimes, despite their increasing commitment to universalism and redistribution over the past seven decades, remain far short of the welfare state ideal, typified by the "gold standard" associated with the Nordic social democracies (Yang, 2013; Lin and Chou, 2007; Holliday, 2005). To be sure, whereas the East Asian welfare regimes are financed through a social insurance mechanism, the northern European welfare states have historically been funded through general taxation revenues, thus contributing to greater redistribution through progressive tax schemes. Though governments in Japan, South Korea, and Taiwan have gradually increased their share of funding to social policy programs, workers' contributions (in the form of social insurance premiums) continue to represent the lion's share of social protection financing. Whereas Nordic welfare programs are universally extended by right of citizenship, East Asia's social insurance regimes are tied to one's employment status, often to one's employer specifically.

Table 1 Social expenditure (% of GDP)

	2000	2010	2020
Japan	16.3	22.1	24.9
South Korea	4.5	8.3	14.4
Taiwan	8.1	9.2	11.9

Sources: https://stats.oecd.org/Index.aspx?datasetcode= SOCX_AGG; http://ws.dgbas.gov.tw

Yet, despite these fundamental differences between the origins and postwar evolution of welfare states in continental Europe and East Asia, most would nonetheless concede that social welfare regimes in Japan, South Korea, and Taiwan expanded significantly over the postwar period. Moreover, as argued in this Element, East Asia's welfare regimes continued to deepen at a time when most welfare states around the world were scaling back or threatening to retrench their social protection commitments, including in the Nordic countries.

Theories of the welfare state, largely developed from the Anglo-European or 'western' experience, inform the pathway that East Asia's welfare regimes took in their evolution. For instance, the logic of industrialism (Wilensky, 1967), a theory that contends welfare reform is intrinsic to industrialization, the sharpening of social class structures, demands for greater inclusion by citizens, and the modernization of the state apparatus is consistent with the East Asian experience in Japan, South Korea, and Taiwan. State-centric theories of social welfare reform (Skocpol, 1995; Immergut, 1992) are especially applicable to East Asia, where strong, autonomous, and capable developmental states guided economic growth and industrialization, as well as social policy change and reform. As this Element contends, the developmental states of postwar Japan, South Korea, and Taiwan experimented with limited social protection schemes and gradually expanded the scope of social insurance coverage to complement their overarching objective to grow and industrialize their economies as well as democratize their polities. Japan, specifically, revived many social insurance schemes that had been introduced decades earlier by the prewar developmental state regime.

The dominant approach to explaining welfare state development, from a more bottom-up or societal point of view, is associated with power resources theory (Esping-Andersen, 1990; Korpi, 1983; Stephens, 1979). Power resources theory essentially contends that the mobilization of the industrial working class through organized labor unions, combined with the presence of a leftist social democratic party, contributes to the deepening of welfare state regimes. Mobilizing the political power of workers and left-leaning parties explains welfare state development. Inspired by Marxist approaches to political economy and drawing from the Anglo-European experiences exemplified by the European welfare states, power resources theory offers a compelling account of welfare state development in many advanced capitalist industrial societies.

However, the East Asian experience of social policy reform and welfare state development did not feature strong leftist parties or especially strong and well-mobilized unions. In fact, as this Element explains, the expansion of social protection schemes in postwar Japan, South Korea, and Taiwan was initiated by historically conservative ruling parties and emerged in political economies in which the left was, and remains, politically marginalized (Wong, 2004a, 2004b). With the exception of a few years during the late 1940s, no ideologically leftist party has governed Japan, South Korea, or Taiwan to this day. In other words, the formation and historical evolution of the welfare state in postwar East Asia, in important ways, reflected a distinctive path.

Organization

This is not a book about social welfare *policy*. It is not intended to be an exhaustive description of the many welfare policies and programs that the governments in Japan, South Korea, and Taiwan introduced, implemented, and expanded over the past several decades. Rather, this Element is about politics and thus seeks to *explain* politically the course of social welfare development in East Asia, drawing on theoretical insights from the welfare state canon to illuminate, though not necessarily explicate fully, East Asia's distinctive experience.

At the core of the analysis is the state. Given the extraordinary role the state played in economic and political development in Japan, South Korea, and Taiwan, it is not surprising the state is the central political actor in the ensuing analysis (Kwon, 2005; Goodman, White, and Kwon, 1998). The state does not operate in a vacuum, however. It adapted and responded to the incentives, constraints, and imperatives of the broader political economic contexts within which they pursued or eschewed welfare reform.

This Element is organized into three sections, with each section corresponding to a specific political economic *context* in the evolution of the East Asian welfare state. Section 1 focuses on the postwar developmental state. In the wake of the Second World War, meeting the pressing urgency to accelerate economic growth and industrialization was the developmental states' overarching priority. In Japan, the developmental state focused on rebuilding its industrial economy. In Korea and Taiwan, it was about building an industrial economy de novo. Social policy was put on the back burner of the policy agenda. Yet, as I explain in this section, the governments in Japan, South Korea, and Taiwan laid (and in the case of Japan, revived) the institutional foundation for occupationally based social insurance schemes. These programs gradually expanded throughout the early postwar period, but always in lock-step with the states' developmental goals to grow and industrialize their economies. I refer to these regimes as *social insurance regimes*.

The second section highlights the impact of democratic transition on the expansion of social welfare in East Asia. Though economic growth and industrial development remained critical priorities, the political pressures of democratic competition compelled political parties to integrate social policy reform into their electoral platforms. The Japanese case is instructive, as it transitioned to democracy much earlier on during the postwar period than did South Korea and Taiwan. Electoral pressures compelled the developmental regime in Japan to accelerate social policy reforms, an argument I introduce in the first section of this Element. Democratic voters, I argue in Section 2, demanded more social welfare in South Korea and Taiwan. Governing and opposition parties were quick to coopt social policy reform agendas into their electoral strategies. As a result, social welfare regimes in democratizing East Asia, first in Japan and subsequently in South Korea and Taiwan, expanded rapidly and became increasingly redistributive in their impact. Importantly, social welfare reform in democratizing East Asia was initiated not by leftist ruling parties, but rather by incumbent conservative "catch-all" parties.

Section 3 brings the analysis to the present, the era of post-industrialism in Japan, South Korea, and Taiwan. East Asia's democratic developmental states have confronted a new political economic context, which has brought it with new challenges to the welfare state (Peng, 2004). Post-industrial pressures have introduced new sources of precarity for nonformal sector workers as well as new vulnerabilities for specific population segments. Women, young people, and the elderly have been especially hard-hit by current political economic realities. Social policy reforms into the 2000s reflect these new labor market pressures and have adapted to address them through labor market policies and targeted social protection programs.

The temptation would be to read the three ensuing sections of this Element as a historical or chronological account of the evolution of welfare regimes in Japan, South Korea, and Taiwan. To be sure, the analysis takes us through the early postwar period, followed by democratic transition in South Korea and Taiwan, and then into the current era of post-industrialism and labor market flexibilization. The temptation to compare the three cases synchronously notwithstanding, the three sections are intended to reflect specific *political economic contexts* – the overarching ethos of developmental statism initially, the political incentives that come with democracy and their effect on social welfare deepening in Section 2, and the current challenges of post-industrialism in the last section of the Element – that have shaped and continue to shape the trajectory of social welfare development in the region.

Thus, while the reader may be tempted to understand the emergence, expansion, and adaptation of the East Asian welfare state chronologically and synchronously across the three cases, it is more analytically fruitful to consider the evolution of social welfare regimes through these *distinct political economic contexts*. Japan, as I argue in this Element, embarked on reforming its social welfare policy regime much earlier than South Korea and Taiwan, just as it industrialized and democratized well before the rest of the East Asia region. But like South Korea and Taiwan, it too evolved through distinct contexts wherein economic imperatives first, followed by democratic pressures and post-industrial challenges, shaped social policy reform. In this regard, the story of the welfare state in East Asia is a story of, and ultimately embedded in, the region's remarkable postwar economic development, its experience with democratic transformation, and currently, efforts to address post-industrial realities.

1 The Developmental State and Social Policy

1.1 Postwar Development and Social Policy

Though Japan, South Korea, and Taiwan are recognized today as global economic powerhouses, they were very poor in the immediate postwar period, during the middle of the twentieth century. Japan was just emerging from the devastation of the Second World War. Its economy severely contracted during the war and Japan's once formidable industrial base was decimated. Though Japan began its economic modernization drive a century before during the mid-nineteenth century, starting with the Meiji reforms, which led to the development of a modern state apparatus and an industrial base, the country's gains were essentially lost as a result of the war. Moreover, the ultimately ill-fated democratic experiment of the 1920s and 1930s, the era of Taisho democracy, proved unsustainable and succumbed to military fascism. In 1945, Japan's economy, society, and polity were in tatters (Dower, 1999). Economic growth and the revival of Japan's developmental state apparatus and its industrial foundation were critical to the country's, and ultimately the region's, postwar recovery.

The Korean War of the early 1950s brought further devastation to the region. Quickly becoming the battle ground for a proxy conflict between the Soviet Union and the United States, the promise of postwar reconstruction stalled. The Korean War cemented the division of the Korean peninsula, with the north ruled by the communists and the southern portion of the peninsula governed by the corrupt Syngman Rhee regime. Political instability and economic stagnation ensued. South Korea's economy, primarily agricultural and barely subsistent at the time, remained sluggish throughout the 1950s and set the stage for Park Chung-hee's military coup in 1961. South Korea was no better off politically and economically by the early 1960s than it had been in the wake of the Second World War.

Meanwhile, the Kuomintang (KMT) nationalists, who fled China during the Chinese civil war, landed on Taiwan in the late 1940s. KMT leaders expected their retreat to Taiwan to be temporary, a short-term stay, with the goal of eventually returning to the mainland and wresting China from the grips of the Communist Party. Brewing ethnic tensions soon after the KMT's arrival between local Taiwanese and Chinese mainlanders who came with the KMT portended political and economic instability. Though the KMT regime eventually had a significant hand in engineering Taiwan's economic developmental state, its early years on Taiwan were rocky.

In short, Korea and Taiwan stumbled out of the gate in finding their political and economic footing after decades of colonial rule. The Japanese colonial regime had been brutal in its political suppression of Korean and Taiwanese society, and extractive in terms of their economies. Colonialism left in its wake backward economies and very weak states. Both Korea and Taiwan were among the poorest economies in the world, and with dim prospects for economic development. Japan, meanwhile, once an industrial power at the beginning of the twentieth century, found itself struggling to regain its economic might in the wake of the devastation of the Second World War.

Under these poor and unstable conditions, a universal and redistributive welfare state was a luxury the immediate postwar governments in Japan, South Korea, and Taiwan could hardly fathom. The European welfare state, which was the gold standard in social welfare democracy at the time, emerged decades earlier and in tandem with capitalist industrialization during the nineteenth and early twentieth centuries. Robust welfare states were associated with the rich industrial economies of continental Europe, and not the developing world (Gough and Wood, 2004). Japan had once been well on its path to industrialization, though the destruction of the prewar regime and the devastation of the war set Japan back decades. In other words, the expectation that poor – and in the cases of Korea and Taiwan, pre-industrial and still largely agricultural – economies in East Asia could afford the introduction of social welfare policies and institutions was far-fetched. Growing a welfare state was an aspiration but not a priority for these East Asian states.

Still, the governments in Japan, South Korea, and Taiwan did introduce some social policy reform during the early postwar period and in subsequent decades throughout the 1960s and 1970s. They did not completely eschew the implementation of and experimentation with *limited* social policies. They were limited in that early social policy reforms during the first few decades after the war, and in the cases of South Korea and Taiwan especially, were far from universal. Organizationally, social protection programs were tied to a person's work and occupation, company-based, and minimally supported by the government. They were primarily limited to workers employed in large industrial firms. Social policy reform at the time was experimental and incremental in nature, especially in South Korea and Taiwan.

In Japan, the introduction of new social policies during the 1950s was actually the revitalization of company-based, prewar social insurance schemes, notably in health insurance and pensions. These social insurance programs were mandated by the government and initially considerably more expansive than in South Korea and Taiwan but delivered by companies to their workers. Japan was way ahead of South Korea and Taiwan in terms of social policy development.

The postwar government in Taiwan implemented very modest social insurance programs, starting with the Labor Insurance scheme in 1950. Modest by design, the early Labor Insurance program was extended only to workers in large firms and covered just 2 percent of Taiwan's population initially. Taiwan's labor insurance scheme gradually and incrementally expanded over time and evolved into a considerably more expansive social protection program decades later. Still, social welfare was tied to workers' employment and not extended as a universal social right. A similar pattern of incremental social policy reform occurred in South Korea. As in Taiwan and Japan, early forms of social insurance in South Korea were dependent on one's work and employment, and, thus initially, limited in their scope of coverage. Occupationally based (or employment-based) social insurance benefited only those who were economically "productive" (Holliday, 2000).

This section examines the origins and early development of social welfare regimes in the region. Social policy reform and gradual experimentation in postwar Japan, South Korea, and Taiwan reflected the political economy of growth and development in the region. Guided by capable, developmentally oriented states, social policy programs were expanded gradually and incrementally. Similar in all three cases was the work-based organization and delivery of social welfare benefits. These were not universal or redistributive social welfare regimes, but rather limited *social insurance regimes* that prioritized economic growth and rapid industrialization.

1.2 Prioritizing Economic Productivity

Social welfare was not the highest priority for the developmental states in postwar Japan, South Korea, and Taiwan; rather, economic growth and industrial development were. Though Japan had introduced some social welfare programs before the war, economic recovery was paramount for the postwar government as well as for the American-led occupation at the time. Domestically, a strong industrial economy generated political legitimacy for the conservative postwar government, as it sought to win the political support of Japan's middle and working classes. From an international point of view, industrial development and economic growth, in addition to the quick revival of some social protection schemes for workers, provided a durable bulwark against communist expansion in the region, vital to US geostrategic interests.

The Cold War logic, which privileged rapid growth in postwar Japan, extended to South Korea and Taiwan as well. Industrial development in South Korea and Taiwan, both economic laggards at the time, was critical to American interests in countering the communist regimes in North Korea and China. As in Japan, prioritizing economic development in South Korea and Taiwan was not just about geopolitics, however. Rapid economic growth became the primary source of "performance legitimacy" for the authoritarian developmental states in South Korea and Taiwan, a way to generate political support for the regimes, or at least stave off intense political opposition (Slater and Wong, 2022). Indeed, between the 1960s and 1980s, Japan, South Korea, and Taiwan were among the fastest growing economies in the world, posting at times near-double-digit annual growth rates. Collectively, they were the engines of the postwar East Asian miracle. Individually, each was an economic dynamo.

Japan's GDP per capita tripled from 1960 to 1980, reaching nearly $26,000 and poised to threaten US economic hegemony by the 1980s. Over the same period, the size of the economy quadrupled in South Korea and Taiwan. South Korea notably joined the OECD club of rich nations in the late 1980s, an impressive developmental milestone and an announcement to the rest of the world that it was an emerging economic power. Taiwan, meanwhile, became one of the world's fastest growing industrial economies and an important manufacturing link in global supply chains. Taiwan's was one of the world's most important exporters by the 1980s, providing skilled labor and vital components to global production chains (Breznitz, 2007). Rapid economic growth and industrialization transformed the economic structure of Japan, South Korea, and Taiwan. Notably, by the end of the century, less than 10 percent of the workforce was employed in the agricultural sector, reflecting a remarkably steep decline in South Korea and Taiwan. By the 1990s, the vast majority of people in all three economies were employed in manufacturing and tertiary sectors.

Economic development in postwar Japan, South Korea, and Taiwan was a regional phenomenon. Japan anchored industrial development in East Asia. It re-emerged as the region's economic leader, quickly rebuilding its domestic industrial champions in the 1950s and becoming a critical source of foreign direct investment into other economies in the region. As its industrial base revitalized and firms diversified their activities into higher value-add sectors, Japanese companies looked to invest in other late developing economies where labor was cheaper though increasingly skilled. Japan was the lead "goose" in the "flying geese" pattern of foreign investment in East Asia (Hatch, 2011). Japan's sunset (declining) industries drove investment into neighboring developing economies. During the 1960s and 1970s, South Korea and Taiwan grew from being among the poorest economies in the world to becoming industrial power-houses by attracting Japanese capital investment, developing their domestic technological capabilities and integrating their firms into regional and global trading networks.

1.2.1 The Developmental State

At the center of East Asia's miracle economies was the developmental state. In all three cases, capable bureaucracies, which also enjoyed a fair degree of political autonomy and policy latitude, directed the allocation of government resources to jumpstart industrial development and to strategically support industrial growth and diversification. The developmental state model, which countries in other regions have attempted to emulate, was born out of specific political economic contexts, first in Japan, then followed by postwar South Korea and Taiwan. The specific historical antecedents that made the developmental state in the region possible cannot be ignored.

For instance, land reform during the late 1940s and 1950s created the economic and political conditions for the emergence of the postwar East Asian developmental state. In all three cases, land reform eliminated the landowning class and eventually redistributed land ownership to farming households. Land reform was especially critical in South Korea and Taiwan. There, land reform exorcised the feudal vestiges of the Japanese colonial landlord system. The state, with the assistance of American planners and advisors, seized and allocated land to farming households. In the Cold War context, redistributing land to peasant farmers, as opposed to collectivizing agriculture (as was the case in communist China), aligned ideologically with the market-conforming policies of the East Asian developmental state.

Land tenure reform contributed to immediate economic benefits to the economy (Looney, 2020). First and foremost, the re-allocation of land resulted in new efficiencies in the agricultural sector and consequently increased prod-uctivity. Farming household incomes grew, especially in South Korea and Taiwan. Surplus agricultural production was sold on domestic, and later, inter-national markets. Critically, foreign exchange earnings from agricultural exports in turn provided an important source of early capital investment into emerging industries, which was much needed in late developers South Korea and Taiwan.

Land and agricultural reform were also critical to the political formation of the developmental state regimes in Japan, South Korea, and Taiwan. In Japan, for instance, agricultural reform cemented for the postwar governing coalition a political foothold among rural voters at the time, a reliable electoral constituency that remained supportive of the ruling Liberal Democratic Party (LDP) for decades to come. Similarly in South Korea and Taiwan, leveling the economic playing field through the redistribution of land generated political legitimacy for the authoritarian regimes in rural areas. The KMT in Taiwan especially needed to win the support of farmers and peasants after its defeat to the Chinese communists on the mainland, due in part to the KMT's lack of appeal in the countryside. In Japan, land reform contributed to the electoral fortunes of ruling parties, while in South Korea and Taiwan it won political support (and quelled an emergent opposition) for the regime.

Politically, land tenure reform destroyed the landlord class, which gained the state considerable political autonomy from the narrowly self-interested grip of the landed elite. The developmental regimes in Japan, South Korea, and Taiwan avoided state capture by the entrenched landed elite. Unlike in other developing economies, notably in Latin America, the East Asian developmental states enjoyed tremendous autonomy from these otherwise historically dominant sectors in society. State autonomy allowed the governments in Japan, South Korea, and Taiwan to develop the technocratic capacity to plan and implement economic development policies, including industrial growth strategies alongside early social policy experiments.

Meritocratic recruitment into the bureaucracy, rather than appointments through political patronage or clientelism, ensured the state bureaucracy in Japan, South Korea, and Taiwan was staffed with the nation's best and brightest technocrats who were generally less susceptible to corruption and graft. Meritocracy contributed to developmental state capacity (Evans, 1995). Not only were the developmental bureaucracies skilled and capable in terms of their policy expertise, but they also wielded tremendous power and authority inside the state apparatus. Economic policy technocrats got things done authoritatively, efficiently, and effectively. The Ministry of International Trade and Industry (MITI) in Japan, for instance, directed industrial policy in a relatively top-down manner, ensuring the line ministries in the bureaucracy were coordinated and worked in concert with MITI directives (Johnson, 1982). The MITI also enjoyed close ties with the ruling Liberal Democratic Party (LDP), which governed Japan uninterrupted from 1955 to 1993, a near-four-decade run during which Japan's economy grew to be the world's second largest, behind only the United States.

In parallel and by emulating the Japanese model, South Korea's Economic Planning Board (EPB) and Taiwan's Council for Economic Planning and

Development (CEPD) emerged as powerful and capable "pilot agencies," as Chalmers Johnson refers to them (1999). The EPB and CEPD devised long-term economic policies and directed industrial development in authoritarian South Korea and Taiwan. Mirroring the political relationship between MITI and the LDP, the developmental state apparatus in South Korea and Taiwan was linked to the governing regimes and their ruling parties (Cheng, 1990). Unlike in postwar democratic Japan, however, where the LDP was repeatedly re-elected and returned to power beginning in the 1950s, the regimes in South Korea and Taiwan were steadfastly anti-democratic and the developmental states' grip on power relied on coercion rather than democratic contestation. In all three cases, however, performance legitimacy was critical to the regimes' ability to maintain political power.

The developmental state enjoyed considerable policy autonomy from dominant social forces, having extensive latitude to design and implement economic policies. In all three cases, the government allocated resources for things that governments normally do, such as human capital development (e.g. investments in the education system) and investments in infrastructure, but also strategically allocating resources for the purposes of developing and growing specific industrial sectors. The developmental state, in other words, "picked winners" in industry and possessed the capacity and control over government resources to essentially "make winners" (Johnson, 1999; Evans, 1995; Wade, 1990).

In South Korea, the most directly interventionist developmental state of the three, the Park Chung-hee regime nationalized the banking sector early on, during the 1960s. Controlling the allocation of credit, the South Korean developmental state was able to execute its industrial policies with the resources to invest in strategic sectors and even firms. The MITI in Japan, less interventionist than in South Korea, nonetheless similarly targeted specific sectors and firms, providing them with economic incentives such as access to credit, procurement contracts, and tax breaks. The developmental state in Taiwan was even less directly interventionist, choosing to employ fiscal incentives in key industrial sectors, instead of directly allocating credit to firms (Cheng, 1990). Irrespective of the differences among them, the capable and autonomous developmental states in East Asia similarly made and rewarded industrial winners through the allocation of capital and other incentives to promising firms in industrial sectors.

The region's economic success was not due solely to strategic industrial policies, but also because the developmental states in Japan, South Korea, and Taiwan collaborated with the business sector, a key feature, incidentally, which contributed to the occupational- or employment-based institutions in their early social policy regimes. According to Peter Evans (1995), the developmental state was "embedded" in industry. For instance, soon after the American occupation ended in the early 1950s, Japan's LDP-led government resurrected through preferential policies the huge industrial combines, the zaibatsu firms, that had driven Japan's prewar industrial economy. The state did not just permit the growth of these proven, winning firms, but rather, it actively grew them through direct interventions. In South Korea, the developmental state similarly facilitated the growth and diversification of a select few chaebol (i.e. conglomerate) firms – national industrial champions – to leverage their scale advantages. About one-fifth of all bank loans were directed to Korea's thirty largest firms. In 1978, South Korea's ten largest chaebols accounted for 34 percent of all manufacturing sales, which doubled to 67 percent six years later in 1984 (Amsden, 1989; see also Woo, 1991). Not surprisingly, companies, and especially large-scale firms, became the organizational backbone of the regimes' early efforts in implementing social insurance programs.

Taiwan's developmental state approached its relationship with the business sector differently, but no less strategically. Rather than concentrate state resources to growing large domestic firms, such as the chaebol firms in South Korea, the KMT instead channeled resources to the state-owned enterprise (SOE) sector. Through a combination of fiscal and industrial policies, rather than direct investments into the private sector, the KMT developmental state indirectly but intentionally facilitated the growth of Taiwan's small and medium-sized enterprises, or SMEs (Cheng, 1990; Haggard, 1990; Wade, 1990). On the one hand, the state-owned enterprises represented the so-called commanding heights of Taiwan's economy, providing key inputs such as steel and energy, while on the other, the diverse and rapidly expanding SME sector was the engine of economic development and employment in Taiwan.

Through a mix of fiscal, regulatory, and industrial policies, the developmental states in Japan, South Korea, and Taiwan transformed their economies from protectionist, import substitution industrialization (ISI) development strategies to export oriented industrialization (EOI). Infant industries were protected through selectively high tariffs, providing firms with access to the domestic market with which they could develop their capabilities to meet international consumer demands. Once domestic firms were able to compete in global markets, the developmentally oriented state targeted incentives to encourage and reward firms to become exporters. The shift from ISI to EOI occurred first in Japan during the 1950s, which led the way when firms ramped up export production to meet American procurement contracts. The shift from ISI to EOI occurred later in South Korea and Taiwan, when firms there plugged into lucrative global supply chains during the 1970s.

Differences notwithstanding among them, the developmentally oriented state in Japan, South Korea, and Taiwan similarly orchestrated economic development through strategic industrial policy interventions. They were market-regarding capitalist regimes, as Chalmers Johnson stresses (1999), supportive of rapid business growth to increase their nation's economic productivity. Yet, they were also developmental regimes that "governed the market," as Robert Wade famously put it (Wade, 1990), picking and making industrial winners to drive economic growth. Their strong states were also critical to weaving their social safety nets.

1.2.2 Growth with Equity

One of the most striking features of the East Asian developmental state experience, in addition to the fact these economies grew so rapidly during the postwar period, was that the distribution of income in Japan, South Korea, and Taiwan remained relatively egalitarian amid periods of high-growth. Contrary to conventional expectations that growth, at least initially, tends to create more socioeconomic inequality, Japan, South Korea, and Taiwan achieved remarkably equitable growth. The Gini coefficient remained relatively egalitarian throughout the 1960s and 1970s, when these economies were growing at nearly double-digit rates. Japan's average Gini between 1965 and 1980 was .247, and Taiwan's was .266. South Korea's Gini coefficient was the most unequal of the three, at an average of .30 between 1965 and 1980 (Solt, 2019). Still, South Korea's Gini was in-line with the most egalitarian Scandinavian countries. South Korea's poverty rate (the incidence of households living in absolute poverty) decreased dramatically from 40.9 percent in 1965 to just 9.8 percent in 1980 (Kwon, 1998).

Several reasons account for the region's pattern of growth with equity. Land reform, first in Japan and later in South Korea and Taiwan during the 1950s, leveled the economic playing field. In Japan, the developmental state destroyed the vestiges of the feudal landlord class and redistributed land to the peasantry. The postwar government in Japan also provided subsidies to small-scale farming households to bolster the agricultural sector. In South Korea and Taiwan, the state, with assistance from American advisors, carried out similarly thorough land and agricultural reform. In Taiwan, the KMT government mandated rent reductions for tenant farmers and later outright seized land and redistributed it to previously landless farmers. By the mid-1960s, almost all of Taiwan's farmable land was owned and tilled by individual farming households. A similar pattern of land reform was carried out in South Korea.

Agricultural reform jumpstarted the development of the agricultural sectors in Japan, South Korea, and Taiwan. Early export earnings in the agricultural sector primed the three economies for their subsequent industrial takeoff, especially in industrial laggards South Korea and Taiwan, where foreign exchange earnings were initially quite low. In addition, gains in agricultural productivity resulted in greater socioeconomic equity by narrowing the income gap between rural and urban households. Land reform in all three places dramatically reduced inequality among households in the countryside. From a political point of view, reducing rural inequality mitigated conflict in the countryside and generated support for the regimes in Japan, South Korea, and Taiwan. In postwar Japan, political support was expressed through the ballot box, while in authoritarian South Korea and Taiwan, the regimes were able to politically mobilize the peasantry in support of the regimes.

To promote growth with equity, the East Asian developmental states also pursued a full-employment industrial growth strategy (Watkins, 1998). The creation of jobs was vital to both economic growth and socioeconomic equity. The commitment to full employment in both rural and urban areas generated wage-earning opportunities. The full-employment strategy mitigated the negative effects of economic re-structuring by absorbing labor surpluses when many left the countryside to find work in urban industries. Japan's Prime Minister Ikeda announced in 1960 his government's ambitious "income doubling plan," which "guarantee[d] that there will not be single hungry or poverty stricken person in the nation" (Kasza, 2011: 194). Central to Ikeda's plan was the implementation of public works projects to create new jobs, put more people to work, and improve industrial productivity (Ide, 2018). In postwar South Korea and Taiwan, rapid industrialization and the growth of competitive manufacturing firms created wage-earning opportunities for an emerging working class, initially in low-skilled labor-intensive manufacturing sectors and later in higher-skilled industries.

Government investments in education and continual labor market upskilling were also critical in developing domestic industries and promoting growth with equity. In addition to ensuring a skilled workforce, human capital investments attracted important sources of foreign direct investment (FDI), which contributed to the growth and maturation of domestic manufacturing industries (You, 1998; World Bank, 1993). Attracting FDI was especially important to late industrial developers South Korea and Taiwan as a way to finance continual industrial upgrading and create new higher-paying employment opportunities. Workers found jobs in Japan, South Korea, and Taiwan.

According to the ILO and the Asian Development Bank, the labor force participation rate in Japan was consistently over 63 percent, while in Korea labor market participation hovered around 60 percent (ILO) during the high-growth period of the 1960s and 1970s. Both countries' labor markets ranked among the strongest of the world's developing economies. Taiwan's labor force participation rate was a bit lower, at just under 60 percent, though this was due to the large number of small, family-based businesses, for which inter-firm mobility was very high. Workers in Taiwan's SME industrial economy found work quickly and consistently.

The developmental state's commitment to a full-employment strategy was critical in reducing unemployment during the period of industrial takeoff. The unemployment rate in Taiwan and Japan was under 2 percent throughout the 1970s, while in South Korea unemployment was just over four percent, still low when compared to other late-developing countries. The key point is that the developmental state, especially in South Korea and Taiwan, achieved growth with equity, not solely through income and wealth redistribution measures typically associated with the welfare state, but by raising the economic floor for the majority of households by ensuring them labor market opportunities to work.

The social impact of growth with equity was important in the region as well. Equitable economic development expanded the size of the middle class (Watkins, 1998), which mitigated the perceptions of social class differences in Japan, South Korea, and Taiwan. Growth with equity muted working-class consciousness and potentially explosive perceptions of relative deprivation. During the 1950s, nearly three-quarters of Japanese survey respondents self-identified as belonging to the middle class. The proportion of those who saw themselves as middle-class grew to over 85 percent of respondents by the mid-1960s (Imada, 1999: 370). Citizens in South Korea and Taiwan similarly overwhelmingly self-identified as belonging to the middle-class rather than the working-class or among the very poor (see Hsiao, 1999). East Asia's experience of rapid growth with equity dampened political demands for progressive social welfare policies.

1.2.3 Marginalizing the Left

Prevailing theories of the welfare state point to the structural transformations brought about by industrial capitalism and specifically the political mobilization of workers to be key drivers of welfare state formation. In the European experience, industrial workers, bound by a shared interest in advancing workers' rights and increasing wages, mobilized their political resources and aligned with leftist political parties to pressure governments to deepen their commitments to social policy reform and ultimately to the formation of a welfare state

(Esping-Andersen, 1990). In industrializing East Asia, however, the development of the political left was stunted, at best, and completely suppressed, at worst. In authoritarian South Korea and Taiwan, the left was explicitly, and oftentimes violently, marginalized from politics. The Cold War context gave little political space in which leftist parties could emerge. Not only did these developmental regimes deliberately pursue strategies to promote rapid growth and accelerate industrialization, they did so while undermining the political left.

Japan is an illustrative example of how the left was ultimately a weakened political force, despite the introduction of democratic reform during the late 1940s. Political conditions initially looked promising for leftist political parties in Japan. The American-led occupation set the stage to implement a democratic constitution in postwar Japan. The 1946 constitution ensured that all political parties competed on a level electoral playing field, a boon to the prospects of multiparty democracy, including for parties on the left. Moreover, fearing that inequality and economic exclusion would destabilize Japan's young and still fragile democracy, the constitution stipulated that all Japanese citizens had the right to work as well as other constitutional commitments to ensuring a decent standard of living (Milly, 1999: 244). In many ways, the 1946 constitution was a progressive constitution.

Indeed, the introduction of a democratic constitution benefited the Japanese Socialist Party (JSP) early on, as voters were drawn to the party's commitment to poverty reduction and redistributive social policies, an appealing platform given the devastation brought by the war years. The JSP importantly represented a departure from the conservative parties, which had driven Japan to fascism during the 1930s. Initially, the JSP was competitive in national elections. In 1947, in fact, the JSP won a plurality of votes, momentarily wresting political power away from the conservative parties that had dominated Japanese politics for decades. The socialist party formed a coalition government that year, and American occupation authorities and conservative parties were forced to reluctantly tolerate the emergence of the political left in democratic Japan.

The JSP's electoral fortunes as a governing party were short-lived, however. The coalition survived only less than one year and collapsed in 1948. The socialists were unable to assemble a workable partnership with any of the other parties in the national Diet (legislature). To make matters worse for the JSP, the political environment became increasingly hostile to leftist parties and their supporters. Conservative parties and industry, on the other hand, benefited from a shift in America's quickly evolving stance on Japan's postwar reconstruction.

Beginning in 1947, American policymakers implemented what historians call its "reverse course" in US foreign policy toward Japan, and to East Asia more generally. As the Cold War escalated and the geopolitical lines were drawn more clearly, the American foreign policy establishment and the occupation authorities in Japan started to marginalize the left in a preemptive effort to contain the spread of communism. They did so in several ways. Occupation authorities permitted the conservative regime to revive the prewar conglomerate firms, despite their earlier stance to dismantle the industrial combines. The effect of this reversal was the re-concentration of industrial and economic power in the hands of a few select industrial champions and allies of the conservative political forces. The conservative government rewarded these industrial giants with procurement contracts, cementing the ties between industry and conservative parties in the Cold War. Furthermore, the Korean War gave Japanese manufacturing industries a significant shot in the arm as American wartime procurement contracts went to Japanese firms.

Leftist political parties, the most significant among them the JSP, saw their influence decline in this increasingly hostile environment. American policymakers feared stability and prosperity would be derailed if the left became too strong politically. Despite the annual Shunto "wage struggle," during which workers pressured employers to increase their compensation, independent labor unions were otherwise politically constrained and limited in their ability to influence government policy (Kume, 1998; Deyo, Haggard, and Koo, 1987; Pempel and Tsuknekawa, 1979). Occupation authorities supported the conservative parties in their bid to reclaim governmental power by gradually restricting workers' rights and choking off the socialist party's support base.

During the mid-1950s, the conservative partisan realignment was completed when the two main conservative parties amalgamated to form the Liberal Democratic Party. The consolidation of the conservative parties further sidelined the JSP and the communist party in the electoral arena. The left in democratic Japan found itself perpetually on the outside looking-in thereafter. The social policy reform agenda, which parties like the JSP were so instrumental in establishing in Japanese electoral politics, was firmly in the hands of the Liberal Democratic Party (LDP).

While the JSP mainstreamed social policy reforms in electoral politics in Japan and continued to play an important role as the opposition party in the early years of Japan's democracy, the fate of the left in postwar South Korea and Taiwan was sealed from the get-go, owing to the authoritarian regimes in place and the Cold War context in which they emerged (Deyo, 1989). South Korea's postwar president, Syngman Rhee, garnered political support from American occupation forces there because of his anti-communist stance. Though his administration drove the South Korean economy further aground, this was the price to pay, as far as the Americans were concerned, in exchange for Rhee's anti-communist, anti-leftist bona fides. The Korean War cemented the South Korean regime's hostility to the left, despite Rhee's developmentally anemic regime. Subsequent authoritarian governments shared a similarly anti-leftist ideology. The authoritarian tools available to the regimes enabled them to politically, often violently, marginalize the left and its supporters.

The Cold War rivalry played out similarly in Taiwan. The KMT regime, which had been defeated by the Chinese communists in the Chinese civil war and fled to Taiwan during the late 1940s, was favored by the United States and by the international community more generally because of its anti-communist stance. Referred to as "Free China," Taiwan was viewed as a vanguard of America's Cold War containment strategy in East Asia. The KMT leader, General Chiang Kai-shek, personified the US anti-communist stance in the region. The KMT imposed Martial Law in 1947, solidifying its authoritarian regime and banned opposition parties altogether, including any political forces on the left.

Labor organizations were politically marginalized in authoritarian South Korea and Taiwan. Between 1963 and 1988, the number of industrial unions remained virtually unchanged in South Korea, for instance. The unionization rate – the percentage of workers enrolled in an organized union – in fact decreased during that time period, from 20.3 percent of workers in 1963 to under 15 percent by 1987 (Song, 1999). Labor union activity in Taiwan was primarily organized within the state-owned enterprise (SOE) sector, meaning worker organizations, where they existed, were infiltrated if not outright controlled by the authoritarian KMT regime. Among non-SOE workers, the unionization rate was even lower than in South Korea, due in part to the KMT's repression of the independent labor movement under Martial Law, but also because of the unique structure of Taiwan's industrial landscape. That the vast majority of private sector firms were SMEs meant the union movement was organizationally fragmented and unable to coalesce any large-scale mobilization (Lee, 2006; Chu, 1998).

1.2.4 Productivist Welfare

The absence of the left and the political marginalization of labor, combined with decades of rapid growth with equity, resulted in a distinct kind of capitalist social policy regime emerging in postwar Japan, South Korea, and Taiwan, and one that challenges conventional understandings of welfare capitalism. Ian Holliday, in his important and much cited 2000 article on welfare state formation in East Asia, introduced the concept of "productivist" welfare capitalism to describe the political economy of social welfare reform in places like Japan, South Korea, and Taiwan, as well as other Asian developmental state regimes. For Holliday, the type of social policy regime that emerged in postwar East Asia reflected the region's overarching priorities in economic growth and industrialization, as well as the state's technocratic capacity to facilitate such development.

As the exemplar of what Holliday calls the "productivist welfare regime," the East Asian model of social protection was not only a social welfare laggard when compared to Europe's welfare states, but a different kind of social policy regime altogether, he contends. According to Holliday, social policy in East Asia's developmental states was fundamentally an "extension of economic policy." Social policy was not intended to be universal in scope and to mitigate socioeconomic risk, nor was its purpose to foster redistribution across the haves and have-nots. Policymakers instead understood that redistributive social welfare policies hampered development and economic growth. Social policy in postwar developmental East Asia was thus "strictly subordinate to the overriding policy objective of economic growth." Holliday goes on to add, "Everything else flows from this: minimal social rights with extensions linked to productive activity, reinforcement of the position of productive elements in society, and state-market-family relationships directed towards growth" (Holliday, 2000: 708). Holliday asserts that the East Asian "productivist" welfare regime represents a "fourth world" of welfare capitalism, appending Esping-Andersen's three world typology.

Because the governments in Japan, South Korea, and Taiwan prioritized economic growth and industrial development, Holliday contends, they allocated resources for social policies and social protection programs to the extent that those *investments directly contributed to economic productivity.* Government expenditures in social programs were an investment in economic growth, in other words, rather than social protection. The purpose of social policy therefore was to promote growth. The developmental state heavily invested in education and labor market upskilling, which it regarded to be a critical driver of productivity and industrial development. South Korea and Taiwan universalized elementary education during the 1960s and expanded access to secondary and post-secondary education throughout the 1970s. The World Bank (1993) credited these human capital investments as the critical source of their economic miracles. Public spending on education alone in South Korea and Taiwan in the 1980s accounted for over 15 percent of government expenditure, while public spending on social protection programs such as poverty relief and unemployment protection was approximately just 1 percent of the budget (see Ku, 1997; Kim and Mo, 1999).

Government spending on redistributive social protection programs, as opposed to productivist investments, was comparatively low during this initial period of rapid economic growth across the region. For instance, in 1980, social policy expenditures by the Japanese government as a share of GDP was just over 10 percent. Meanwhile, the OECD average was double that, at about 20 percent of GDP. Government spending on social policies in Taiwan was just 3.8 percent of GDP, and in South Korea, even more paltry at 2.5 percent (Chan, 2008: 303). Rather than government-funded social programs, the social safety net in East Asia primarily comprised family and kinship networks, in addition to selective company-based welfare social insurance schemes.

1.3 The Social Insurance Regime

Growth with equity and the marginalization of the left weakened bottom-up political pressures for expanded social welfare, as power resources theories of the welfare state would expect. And yet, the governing regimes in Japan, South Korea, and Taiwan did not completely eschew social policy reform. Importantly, the governments experimented with various social insurance schemes, which offered limited social protection for some, though not all workers (Peng and Wong, 2008; Wong, 2003; Holliday, 2000). To a very limited degree, the governments administered and fiscally contributed to the social insurance programs. In most schemes, social insurance programs were managed by firms and offered limited social protection benefits to their workers. In this regard, the postwar developmental states were not welfare regimes but rather *social insurance regimes*.

1.3.1 Japan

Japan was the earliest adopter of social insurance among the three cases. Mimicking the Bismarckian social insurance model of nineteenth-century Germany, the Japanese government introduced its first social insurance program in 1927, which at the time was a modest health scheme that covered industrial workers employed at large firms. The initial health insurance program, and later Japan's first pension scheme, provided limited benefits to industrial workers and required significant contributions from employers and employees. Fiscal contributions to the insurance schemes from the government were insignificant. Furthermore, socioeconomic redistribution was limited due to the size and scope of the company-based insurance pools. The number of social insurance programs gradually expanded and the schemes were tinkered with during the 1930s. However, the Japanese government made no significant structural changes to the company-based social protection system and the extension of benefits remained far from universal throughout the prewar period (Kasza, 2011). The structural legacy of the social insurance model would have a significant impact on the evolution of welfare state formation in postwar Japan and in the region.

Gregory Kasza notes that the early emergence of social policy schemes during the late 1920s and 1930s coincided with Japan's rise as a regional industrial power and with the gradual deterioration of its imperial democratic institutions, setting the stage for militaristic fascism. In the late 1930s, the government created its first Ministry of Welfare to galvanize and nationalize various social insurance schemes. As Kasza observes, early social policy reforms and efforts to steer reform through the welfare ministry "embodied a war-related human resources perspective" rather than social protection. Social welfare was intended to prepare and mobilize the nation for impending war, reflected in nationalist slogans such as "all people are soldiers" and "healthy soldiers, healthy people" (Kasza, 2002: 423, 424). Japan's nascent social insurance regime was a tool, Kasza argues, for mobilizing nationalism and the fascist regime's efforts at nation-building. The introduction of social policy was intended to foster wartime national cohesion, not social protection for the vulnerable.

The devastation of the Second World War and Japan's eventual surrender ended the fascists' reign. Collaborating with the US occupation, the interim government installed a new democratic constitution in 1946. The American-led occupation aimed to rebuild Japan. In addition to guiding political reform, occupation leaders worked with local policymakers to revive Japan's industrial economy. Occupation leaders also insisted the government revive its prewar social policies and expand its social welfare commitments to facilitate balanced economic growth, for fear the prewar socioeconomic divisions might reappear and derail Japan's development. Political pressure and the electoral appeal of the JSP were especially concerning for both the conservative parties and the American-led occupation. Consequently, the postwar government, which was dominated by conservative political parties that were historically hostile to social welfare programs, gradually increased the scope of Japan's nascent social safety net during the late 1940s and early 1950s to head off any electoral threat from the left.

Postwar Japan's commitment to gradually expand the role of the state in weaving together a social safety net continued into the 1950s and beyond, a process that was led, ironically and importantly, by conservative parties and not the socialists (Miura, 2012). The political left, though instrumental in shaping Japan's early postwar social policy reform agenda, was not the key driver in deepening Japan's social insurance regime during the 1950s and 1960s; rather, conservative parties, notably the LDP after its formation in 1955, had a much more significant impact on social policy reform. Despite its conservative ideological roots, the LDP embraced a more expansive social welfare regime. Social policies were popular among voters, and it made sense for the LDP to position itself as a catch-all party, appealing to both employers and workers, conservatives and progressive voters.

The LDP marginalized the political left in electoral politics, while coopting its social policy reform agenda (Milly, 1999). Unlike in authoritarian South Kore and Taiwan, electoral politics mattered a great deal in postwar Japan and influenced the government's priorities. Deepening its commitment to social protection won the ruling party considerable political support and votes at the ballot box. In 1955, the start of the LDP's nearly four-decade-long reign as Japan's ruling party, the government announced plans to introduce a comprehensive health insurance program, which it achieved six years later in 1961. The LDP expanded health insurance coverage to include workers in not only large industrial firms, reviving the prewar social insurance regime, but extended it to small firms as well as to those employed in agricultural sectors (Campbell and Ikegami, 1998). That same year, the government reintroduced its prewar pension schemes, and, as with health insurance, expanded old-age income security coverage to all employees, including self-employed workers.

It is important to note that despite the democratically elected LDP government's gradually increasing role in legislating, administering and even financially contributing to various social protection programs, the health and pension schemes, Japan's two most significant social programs, and remained contributory social insurance programs. Social insurance rather than tax-funded social welfare schemes continued to be administered by firms for the most part, reinforcing the company-based features and occupational-bias of the growing social safety net. The expansion of benefits and coverage in health insurance and pension schemes in 1961, importantly, did not involve the structural transformation of the existing social insurance system, but, rather, expanded the scope of coverage to include more workers and their employers. Social policy reforms introduced in the 1960s expanded the scope and generosity of the social safety net in Japan but did not transform it.

The legacies of the prewar social insurance schemes left a deep imprint on what was viable in the postwar period. The provision of social insurance, with the exception of smaller insurance programs for self-employed workers (including those employed in farming and fishing sectors), largely remained with companies. The state's fiscal responsibility did not increase significantly, as workers and their employers contributed most (up to 90 percent) of the insurance premiums. As before, firms collected and pooled medical insurance and pension premiums, and companies, and not the government, were responsible for the provision of worker benefits. Moreover, insurance funds were not integrated or pooled among firms, which limited the amount of risk- and financial-pooling. The lack of pooled insurance minimized redistribution across different groups of wage earners. Companies managed their own risk and provided social protection to *their own* workers.

The key point is that companies were at the center of the social insurance regime in Japan, and not the state. While the government mandated and regulated the social insurance schemes, it was not the main financial contributor nor insurance provider. Not surprisingly, the combination of lifetime employment at a single firm and selective benefits from the company's social insurance schemes strengthened workers' loyalties as well as their dependency on the firm (Estevez-Abe, 2008; Estevez-Abe, Iverson, and Soskice, 2001). The deeply entrenched firm-centric nature of Japan's social insurance system meant that workers received different benefits and contributed different amounts depending on the specific company at which they were employed. Japan's decentralized model of "company welfare" and company-based insurance schemes resulted in an increasingly expansive, yet *stratified*, social safety net. Employees in large firms enjoyed far more generous benefits than those employed in smaller companies.

1.3.2 South Korea

The South Korean developmental state introduced a limited social insurance system in the early 1960s. In 1963, the authoritarian regime passed the Health Insurance Act, which opened the way for firms to provide social protection benefits to their workers. Unlike in Japan, however, the Korean insurance program was voluntary, requiring firms to opt-in. South Korea's earliest health insurance scheme featured multiple insurance "carriers" (or funds) organized at the level of the firm. The decentralized and fragmented health insurance programs provided very few benefits to workers. The 1963 health insurance scheme was not intended to provide comprehensive medical care coverage. Later that year, the government legislated the Industrial Accident Insurance Act, another employer-organized social insurance scheme, but which was aimed specifically at workplace injuries. Because of the limited scope of benefits in the 1963 medical insurance program, the new industrial accident scheme made the voluntary health program redundant and the government scrapped the medical insurance program soon after (Wong, 2004a; Kwon, 1999).

South Korea's authoritarian developmental state continued to experiment with the social insurance model. During the early 1970s, the Park Chung-hee regime legislated new social policy programs, notably with the passage of the 1973 National Pension Act. Similar to the fate of the short-lived health insurance program a decade earlier, the government mothballed the pension program soon after it was introduced. The OPEC price spikes of the early 1970s disrupted economic development and the government abandoned its social policy experiments to re-commit to a growth-first strategy.

During the mid-1970s, after South Korea's economy rebounded from the OPEC crisis, the Ministry of Health and Social Affairs (MHSA), a bureaucratic proponent of expanding the state's role in social protection provision, led the government's renewed effort to legislate a medical insurance program. The 1976 Health Insurance Act, which was the result of that effort, resembled the 1963 legislation, specifically the adoption of a social insurance model in addition to the decentralized organization of the insurance funds. One key difference, however, was that the 1976 program was mandatory for all large firms employing over 500 workers. Large firms were required to implement a company-organized medical insurance carrier (fund), into which employees and employers contributed insurance premiums.

During the first stages of the program's rollout, hundreds of separate company-based insurance funds were introduced. Benefits provided through the separate health insurance schemes differed among the companies and thus premium rates varied between firms as well. Similar to Japan's decentralized company-based social insurance program, South Korea's health insurance schemes differentiated large firms from SMEs and stratified worker benefits based on the company they were employed with. Workers in large industrial firms were not only paid higher wages, they received more social protection benefits than their counterparts employed in smaller firms (Yang, 2013; Song, 2003). And like in Japan, there was no risk- or financial-pooling across the funds, meaning little redistribution among them.

The South Korean government gradually expanded coverage in the health insurance system (Ringen, 2011). In 1978, the state launched the publicly funded government employee medical insurance program and established a single insurance carrier for civil servants. The government employee insurance fund operated parallel to (i.e. separate from) the multiple corporate medical insurance funds. The company-based insurance program expanded in 1980 to include firms with 300 and more employees and expanded again a year later to medium-sized enterprises employing 100 and more workers. Soon after, the government experimented with pilot programs in medical insurance coverage for self-employed workers (Son, 2002).

Only 9 percent of workers benefited from medical insurance coverage when the program was first initiated in 1976, though by 1981, enrollment had increased to 30 percent of the workforce. As the health insurance system expanded to include more firms, the number of insurance carriers increased too, which resulted in a complicated and decentralized patchwork of company-managed funds with no financial or risk-pooling among them (Wong, 2004a). Similar to Japan, the increasingly expansive social insurance regime in South Korea differentiated company schemes, stratified welfare benefits, and undermined worker solidarity.

1.3.3 Taiwan

The KMT government in Taiwan, not unlike the ruling regimes in Japan and South Korea, elected to develop its social policy regime based on the social insurance model. However, rather than copy the company-based approach featured in postwar Japan and South Korea, the KMT government managed the social insurance schemes. In 1950, the government introduced a very modest labor insurance scheme that was extended to workers in firms employing twenty or more employees. The program was mandatory for all firms. Employees and employers paid-in to the insurance scheme, with the employer contributing three-quarters of the premium. The government administered the insurance scheme and allocated resources to manage the labor insurance fund, though it did not directly contribute to workers' premiums (Ku, 1997).

The 1950 labor insurance program was a pilot program, and very few workers enrolled. The benefits were modest, limited to basic health provisions and with an emphasis on workplace-related injuries. The program's reach was quite modest as well because Taiwan's economy at the time featured prominently micro family-based enterprises, almost all of them employing fewer than twenty workers. The labor insurance scheme first expanded its scope of coverage in 1953, requiring firms with ten or more employees join the program. Military personnel were included that year, though they were covered under a separate insurance fund. In 1958, the government legislated the Labor Insurance Act, turning the early pilot program into actual government policy. It also introduced the government employee insurance scheme, supported by a separate fund under the state's administration. Notably, the 1958 legislation harmonized the benefits package provided by the various insurance schemes, including standardized "bundled benefits" for work-related injuries, old-age income security, disability, and medical care (Son, 2002, 2001).

The Taiwan government increased its social policy commitments throughout the 1970s, adding new social protection programs, including smaller initiatives in child welfare, education as well as growing its commitments to social assistance to address poverty. A landmark reform came in 1979 when the

KMT proposed and passed significant revisions to the labor insurance program. Coverage was extended to small enterprises with five or more employees, which dramatically increased the number of workers enrolled in the program. The 1979 changes also resulted in adjustments to several eligibility requirements, including, importantly, shortening the length of tenure for workers to claim old-age benefits. During the 1980s, the KMT government again experimented with pilot programs to extend labor insurance schemes to farmers and fishermen. A new labor insurance fund was created to enroll schoolteachers as well. At the same time, the KMT rapidly expanded the government employee insurance program to include retired civil servants in addition to nonworking dependents of government workers (Wong, 2004a; Ku, 1997).

1.4 The Political Economy of Social Policy Reform

The origins and evolution of the social insurance regimes in Japan, South Korea, and Taiwan were in many respects strikingly similar. Japan led the way, as it did in many regards in the region, by adopting the German social insurance model, initially during the prewar period in the 1920s and 1930s and later reviving and then expanding it after the war. The authoritarian developmental states in Korea and Taiwan learned from the Japanese example by implementing more modest and limited insurance schemes in the postwar period. While government played an administrative and legislative role in gradually expanding the scope of social insurance coverage, in all three cases, the state contributed little financially. Workers and their employers were the primary contributors to the insurance programs. Moreover, the social insurance regimes did not integrate or structurally consolidate what were decentralized insurance funds, notably in South Korea and Japan, hence minimizing socioeconomic redistribution among workers and in many ways further stratified them.

Ito Peng and Joseph Wong (2008) contend that the "institutional purpose" of the postwar social insurance regime in East Asia was not to facilitate redistribution nor to promote greater equity, but rather to benefit the economically "productive" sectors of society (see also Fleckenstein and Lee, 2017). In other words, the limited role that government played in directly contributing to social welfare was intentional, reflecting what Ian Holliday characterizes as East Asia's distinctively *productivist* welfare state. From an economic development point of view, investments in education and social protection were intended to bolster the productivity of workers. The productivist logic was most evident in South Korea and Taiwan, where those who were not economically productive, such as dependent children and older retirees, were excluded from the company-based social insurance schemes. Informally employed workers were ineligible for social insurance coverage. Assistance for the poor and unemployment in all three cases was miniscule to start with and declined over time. The gradual implementation of the social insurance regimes in postwar East Asia was informed by an overarching economic logic, an "institutional purpose" as Peng and Wong put it, that privileged the recovery of Japan's industrial base and rapid development in South Korea and Taiwan.

Importantly, the introduction of social policy reform in postwar East Asia, or reintroduction in the case of Japan, was largely led by a conservative elite. The expansion of social insurance in all three cases was instigated initially and later expanded by conservative ruling parties, and in South Korea and Taiwan, by ideologically conservative authoritarian regimes. East Asia's early experience in social policy reform was distinctive in this regard. There was a political logic to the development of the social insurance regime in Japan, South Korea, and Taiwan. These were not, as Holliday and others note, politically "unaccountable" regimes (Holliday, 2000: 715; White and Goodman, 1998: 15). Indeed, political support was critical to the governing parties in all three places.

The conservative LDP needed to win votes to stay in power, including from voters who might support leftist parties such as the JSP. Meanwhile, the authoritarian regimes in South Korea and Taiwan, while they did not contest in democratic elections, also needed political support, or in the least, minimize opposition to stay in power. Though they possessed the repressive apparatus of the authoritarian state to quell dissent, the regimes in South Korea and Taiwan also looked to curry political support through their performance legitimacy. The authoritarian regimes did not need to win elections, as the LDP did in Japan, but they did need to generate political support.

Political imperatives, and specifically the imperative to earn performance legitimacy and to win political support, informed *when* social policy reforms occurred. Politics shaped the timing and sequencing of social policy reform (for Japan, see Calder, 1988). The authoritarian regimes, for instance, introduced and later expanded their social insurance schemes during times of political crisis. In Taiwan, the most significant expansions to the Labor Insurance program occurred first when the KMT initially consolidated its authoritarian power during the early 1950s and again when the regime confronted an emerging political opposition during the late 1970s (Ku, 1997). In both instances, social policy reform was used to address political challenges. Similarly, South Korea's Park Chung-hee dictatorship reintroduced a health insurance scheme during the early 1970s first, and further expanded the program's coverage to government employees shortly after. Both reforms came about when Park was trying to solidify his authoritarian reign. In the early 1980s, President Chun Doo-hwan expanded the government's social insurance programs precisely at the time when his regime was on politically shaky ground. In other words, the gradual and timely expansion of social policy programs was deployed as an effective instrument for managing the regimes' political crises.

The political logic of social policy reform was not only evident in the timing of social policy reform but also the sequencing of who the beneficiaries were in authoritarian South Korea and Taiwan. Industrial workers were among the first to be covered in the social insurance schemes, followed by government employees and civil servants, as well as military personnel, all of whom represented important sources of political support for the authoritarian regimes. Meanwhile, those less likely to present a political threat or who were not a political priority, notably farmers or self-employed workers, were integrated much later. Dependents, such as the elderly or other family members, were excluded.

In Japan, the JSP's early electoral success elevated the social welfare reform agenda into the electoral mainstream. Parties on the left amplified voters' concerns about economic recovery as well as the distributive consequences of rapid economic growth. Conservative parties, and later the LDP, tacked to the political center, coopting the left's social welfare policy agenda. Fashioning itself as a "catch-all" party, the conservative LDP met political and electoral pressures by adopting and implementing significant social welfare reforms. Efforts to win voter support accelerated the development of a more robust social safety net.

In all three cases, political pressure mattered to the origins of the welfare state in East Asia. But political pressure in a democratic developmental state, such as in postwar Japan, is different than in authoritarian developmental states. Electoral imperatives compel governments to introduce social protection programs and politically incentivize them to expand them more quickly and more generously, as the case of postwar democratic Japan demonstrates. The impact of democratic political pressure on social policy reform in South Korea and Taiwan is explored more fully in the following section.

2 Democratization and Social Welfare

2.1 Democracy and the Welfare State

Social protection programs in postwar Japan, South Korea, and Taiwan were productivist by design, subordinated to, and ultimately in support of the developmental states' overarching priority for economic productivity and growth. Social protection, especially in authoritarian South Korea and Taiwan, was limited in coverage and far from universal; social policy programs were not, nor were they ever intended to be, redistributive. Moreover, the governments in South Korea and Taiwan contributed little financially to the social safety net, relying primarily on company welfare schemes to deliver social protection for their employees and insurance premiums paid by workers.

This began to change in the 1980s and 1990s in *democratizing* South Korea and Taiwan, a critical period during which the limited social insurance regimes described in the previous section committed to *welfare state deepening*. Democratizing South Korea introduced a pensions program and universalized its medical insurance program during the late 1980s, followed by significant structural reform to the health insurance system in the late 1990s. The democratizing KMT regime in Taiwan, meanwhile, experimented with expanded old-age income security schemes in the 1980s. Most notably, the government implemented a comprehensive and universal National Health Insurance (NHI) program in 1995. Later that decade, the democratically elected KMT government introduced an ambitious unemployment insurance scheme, a policy which was enacted into law a few years later in 2003, not by the KMT, but rather by the former opposition Democratic Progressive Party (DPP), after its party's candidate won the presidency in 2000. Social policy reform became a priority for contending political parties in democratizing East Asia.

The timing and impact of the reforms were significant. Social policy reforms in democratizing South Korea and Taiwan were *intended* to be universal and not limited to those who were employed and economically productive. Nonworking dependents, such as the unemployed, children, and the elderly, were gradually included as part of these reform efforts. Revamped as well as new health and pensions programs were designed to be more redistributive in their impact. Social welfare programs consolidated formerly decentralized insurance pools and redistributed benefits more inclusively and across a wider range of recipients. Finally, government financial contributions to the labor insurance and health insurance schemes, and specifically for self-employed workers and nonworking dependents, increased considerably beginning in the 1980s and accelerated over the 1990s.

In terms of timing, democratic transition in South Korea and Taiwan coincided with welfare state deepening, reflecting the political logic introduced at the end of the first section of this Element. Data on government expenditures confirm the connection between democratization and welfare state deepening. For example, overall social spending by the government – public funds allocated for social policy programs – in South Korea increased from 12.4 percent of the government's bill in 1985 to 17.8 percent in 1994. Over that period, government spending on social security and welfare programs specifically nearly doubled from 5.2 percent to 9.3 percent of the central government's total expenditures (Kim and Mo, 1999: 79). Similarly in Taiwan, the government increased its share of social spending over the course of the 1990s, when the regime began to democratize. Between 1992 and 2000, social welfare expenditure as a percentage of total government spending grew from 14.7 percent to 25.3 percent. The most significant spending increases were in the state's fiscal contributions to social insurance programs, in addition to new resources dedicated to welfare relief for the poor (Lin, 2018: 404; Ku, 1997). The democratizing governments increased their commitments to new social protection programs, over and above their earlier investments in education and labor market upskilling.

In this section, we examine more closely the impact of democratization on social policy reform in East Asia, with a specific focus on political transitions in South Korea and Taiwan. Just as the overarching priority of productivism and economic growth shaped the course of social policy reform during the early postwar period in the region, the introduction of democracy – first in Japan beginning in the 1940s and into the 1950s, and later in Korea and Taiwan during the late 1980s – had a profound effect on the *democratic politics* of social policy reform. As the case of postwar Japan illustrates, democratic politics and specifically electoral incentives matter when it comes to the political logic of social welfare reform in East Asia.

Democracy fundamentally alters the political game, and with it the incentives for the developmental states to deepen their commitments to social welfare deepening. Stephan Haggard and Robert Kaufman (2009) characterize democratization in Asia as a critical "realignment" in the political economy of welfare state development. Wong (2004a) and others (Shim, 2020; Kwon, 1999; Ku, 1997) similarly identify democratization as a critical political juncture that steered, first, Japan, and later South Korea and Taiwan, on a course toward welfare state deepening.

Democracy's impact on social policy reform mattered in many ways. Democratic transition opened up political space to new actors. Civil society groups, once excluded from mainstream politics, were critical in mobilizing support for reform. In some instances, civil society actors successfully resisted efforts by the government to scale-back or retrench social welfare programs (Wong, 2003). Workers increasingly formed independent labor organizations to pressure and push for more egalitarian social and economic policies, especially in South Korea and Taiwan where democracy arrived much later during the late 1980s and early 1990s.

The introduction of democracy in East Asia entailed new political "rules of the game" and created new channels of political influence as well as new modes of political mobilization. Whereas under authoritarianism, contentious politics and bottom-up mobilization were routinely suppressed by the autocratic regime, under democracy, newly enfranchised actors gained influence over policy outcomes through a variety of means and mechanisms, from direct lobbying of the bureaucracy, to electoral campaigns which mobilized around social policy platforms, to forming alliances and coalitions with political parties that have to compete for power at the ballot box and the elected legislatures (Wong, 2005).

Democratic transition changed not only the rules of the game but also the objective of the political game. Authoritarian regimes ultimately maintain their power by suppressing dissent and opposition, often violently. Democratic governments, on the other hand, can only attain political power by *winning* support through electoral contests (Wong, 2004a). Thus, whereas authoritarian regimes are incentivized to eliminate or suppress their opposition, democratic parties are incentivized to generate electoral support. Social welfare reform and increasing the government's role in welfare state deepening, I contend in this section, proved to be a winning formula for vote-seeking, democratic governments in Japan, South Korea, and Taiwan. Political power in democracies is won at the ballot box.

2.2 Democratization and Social Policy

Whereas democratic transition in Japan was deeply influenced by the postwar American occupation, democracy arrived later in South Korea and Taiwan through domestic democratic transitions. Also unlike in Japan where the fascist wartime government was forced to surrender in the wake of the world war, the authoritarian incumbent ruling parties in South Korea and Taiwan survived their democratic transitions, and in fact remained in political power after winning founding elections. Incumbent parties thrived in democracy, in part, because of their evolution from limited productivist social policy regimes to becoming more robust, universalist, and increasingly redistributive welfare regimes. Like the LDP in postwar democratic Japan, the incumbent governing parties in democratizing South Korea and Taiwan enhanced their democratic durability – and indeed, their enduring *electability* – because of their instincts for political survival and their strategies for winning elections in democracy. Social welfare reform was a winning strategy.

2.2.1 Democratizing East Asia

To explain how democracy impacted social policy reform in South Korea and Taiwan, we need to first understand how democratic transition unfolded in the two former authoritarian states. In both places, democratization was initiated by the incumbent authoritarian regime. As Slater and Wong contend (2013, 2022), the authoritarian rulers "conceded" democracy from a position of strength, with the expectation that instigating democratic reform would not spell their political demise but would instead allow the incumbent ruling parties to remain in power as democratically elected governments.

In Taiwan, growing opposition forces from within society signaled to the KMT regime that its once unassailable grip on power had begun to wane by the mid-1980s. In 1986, the KMT's burgeoning opposition proclaimed the formation of the Democratic Progressive Party (DPP). Technically illegal, as Taiwan was under Martial Law at the time, the formation of the DPP challenged the authoritarian KMT regime. Most observers at the time assumed the KMT would crack down on the DPP and suppress the emerging opposition; after all, the KMT had proved to be, at times, a ruthless and violent regime when it came to preserving its dictatorial hold on power (Chao and Myers, 1998).

President Chiang Ching-Kuo, however, refrained from sweeping up opposition leaders and suppressing the DPP. The KMT allowed the opposition party to form and compete in supplementary elections soon after. In 1987, the ruling party ended Martial Law and started to put into place other liberalizing political reforms, including full and freer elections, expanded freedom of the press and freedom of association, the space to politically mobilize in civil society, and the right to form official opposition parties. President Chiang noted in 1986 that the "times have changed; events have changed; trends have changed. In response to these changes, the ruling party must adopt new ways to meet this democratic revolution" (cited in Moody, 1992). During the early 1990s, reform-oriented leaders from the KMT and the opposition DPP convened the National Affairs Conference and together negotiated the blueprint for Taiwan's democratic transition.

Democracy in Taiwan did not emerge from the detritus of a failed autocratic regime. The dictatorship did not collapse under the weight of its illegitimacy, as we see in many other third wave democracies (Huntington, 1991). Rather, the KMT, which had directed Taiwan's postwar economic miracle, was electorally popular during the 1980s. The authoritarian regime conceded democracy when the KMT remained strong and confident that it could win political power through democratic elections, which it did handily throughout the 1990s. The KMT chose to democratize during relatively "good times," when it remained a credible ruling party (Haggard and Kaufman, 1995).

The conservative authoritarian regime in South Korea considered a similar democratic concession around the same time, which initiated its democratic transformation. After decades of ruling through brutal repression right through the mid-1980s, the authoritarian Democratic Justice Party (DJP) chose to democratize when it confronted growing opposition from civil society, but when it remained relatively strong. In the summer of 1987 and amid nationwide protests pushing for political reform (Lee, 2007), General Roh Tae-Woo, the handpicked successor to the outgoing dictator Chun Doo-Hwan, announced unexpectedly the regime's plans to introduce full democratic elections. The December 1987 presidential contest followed by full National Assembly elections in the spring of 1988 were to be free and fair.

Echoing Chiang Ching-Kuo's observations of Taiwan, Roh conceded that "there [wa]s a strong wind of change blowing over the country," and that South Korea must usher in "an era of mature democracy" (cited in Lee and Campbell, 1994; see also Cotton, 1989). Similar to Taiwan's KMT, the incumbent ruling party in Korea enjoyed considerable strengths when the DJP initiated democratic transition in the summer of 1987. Notwithstanding mass protests, the DJP was not a regime on the brink of imminent collapse. It was fledgling, to be sure, but it was not on its last legs. Recall that the economy at the time was very strong. South Korea had just joined the OECD. The authoritarian regime in South Korea, despite its horrific legacy of authoritarian rule, in fact remained quite popular, having accumulated considerable performance legitimacy through its economic development track record. Roh Tae-Woo ended up winning the founding democratic presidential election in 1987, with just over one-third of the vote. The DJP managed to control a plurality of seats in the National Assembly after the 1988 spring election. The incumbent ruling party took its hits, but it was still in power.

In both Taiwan and South Korea, the incumbent authoritarian regimes were not weak regimes when they democratized, and they were certainly not weak governments after their democratic transitions. Still, despite the two regimes' inherited strengths, the DJP and KMT, similar to the LDP in Japan, acknowledged the need to shore up their democratic political support if they were to stay dominant in democracy. Their earned performance legitimacy – inherited strengths and credibility in managing the economy in the postwar period – was not inexhaustible. As Slater and Wong put it, theirs were developmental states which had fostered demanding "developmental voters" who sought more from their democratically elected governments (Slater and Wong, 2022).

In other words, past developmental records – good enough for the KMT and DJP to win the founding democratic elections – were likely not enough to retain their dominance in subsequent contests; at least that was not a bet either of the ruling parties wanted to make over the longer term. No longer able to rely on the repressive tactics of the authoritarian state to fend off their challengers, the incumbent ruling parties needed to win electoral votes. In short, they needed winning platforms.

2.2.2 Deepening the Welfare State

As noted in the previous section, the conservative ruling party in Japan, the LDP, deliberately shifted its policy platform to embrace a more robust welfare state beginning as early as the 1950s. Having fended off an early challenge by the JSP during the late 1940s, the newly formed LDP saw it needed to appeal to a broader voter base, including those who had supported the Japanese Socialist Party (JSP). To make it more appealing to voters, the LDP coopted aspects of the socialist's agenda, including deepening its commitment to social policy reform. The Policy Affairs Research Council (PARC), essentially the party's internal policy brain trust, proposed a new social policy vision that committed the LDP to constructing a "welfare state," a remarkable departure from the LDP's conservative heritage (Muira, 2012: 47).

Democracy's arrival in early postwar Japan accelerated the government's commitment to expanding the social safety net. In addition to extending a raft of economic benefits to farmers and urban workers, LDP Prime Minister Ikeda introduced the "income doubling" plan in 1960, a poverty reduction strategy that depended on increasing employment opportunities through public works investments. The government stimulated the labor market by direct interventions to generate employment. Its reform efforts did not end there. A year later, in 1961, the LDP extended pension and medical insurance benefits to workers in smaller firms, as well as to farmers and eventually to self-employed workers. Responding to electoral pressures, the LDP essentially tacked toward the ideological center, becoming a "catch-all" party that credibly appealed to broad swathes of Japanese society rather than its narrower base of historically conservative voters.

The ruling parties in South Korea and Taiwan responded to new democratic pressures by positioning themselves as catch-all parties, like the LDP, by deliberately incorporating social policy reform agendas into their winning electoral platforms. But whereas democracy arrived earlier in Japan, democratic transition in South Korea and Taiwan came later, and so too the impact of democratization on social welfare reform.

The case of democratizing South Korea is instructive. In early 1988, one month before the founding National Assembly elections that March, the DJP expanded health insurance coverage to rural self-employed workers. Responding to months of protest by farmers demanding a public subsidy to offset the insurance premiums, the government increased its share of medical insurance financing. Not only did the medical insurance scheme expand its coverage, fiscal contributions to protecting farmers increased as well. From a political point of view, the timing of reform was not coincidental. The incumbent ruling party looked to gain an electoral advantage in the countryside in advance of the spring 1988 legislative contest. Given the seat bonus in rural electoral districts (i.e. the overrepresentation of rural districts in the National Assembly), expanding benefits to farmers proved an effective winning strategy for the incumbent party. The DJP expanded medical insurance coverage to urban self-employed workers a year later, in 1989, again to shore up its bases of political support (Wong, 2004a).

Expansion did not mean greater redistribution. The decentralized insurance system still limited risk- and financial-pooling among insurance enrollees. South Korea's fragmented medical insurance scheme comprised several hundred separate heath insurance funds, which minimized the redistributive impact of the social insurance system. Moreover, because the insurance funds were administered separately and usually at the company-level, insurance premium rates and benefits varied widely among the different schemes. The decentralized organization of the social insurance system exacerbated socioeconomic inequalities, as described in Section 1.

Fragmented social insurance was not always the government's intention. As early as the 1970s, years before the universalization of health insurance coverage, progressive bureaucrats in the then Ministry of Health and Social Affairs (MHSA) advocated for medical insurance fund consolidation. They proposed to merge the disparate, company-based health insurance funds into a single insurance carrier, both to pool and to redistribute risk and benefits among all enrollees. Policymakers at the time (during the 1970s) resisted these reform efforts, as they were concerned about the negative economic effects of welfare state expansion.

The democratically elected government in South Korea, however, pursued health insurance integration to promote greater inclusion and redistribution among beneficiaries. The proposal to consolidate the medical insurance system gained momentum during the late 1990s, in the wake of the 1997 Asian Financial Crisis. Former opposition leader Kim Dae-Jung was elected to the presidency in December of 1997, in part because of his appeals to voters and civil society organizations to support his more progressive economic and social policy platform. Social welfare policy deepening was near the top of his agenda, including, notably, the integration of health insurance funds (Hwang, 2012; Holliday, 2005; Wong, 2004a). Supported by civil society, elected politicians and government bureaucrats, the Ministry of Health and Welfare (MOHW) proposed the landmark medical insurance integration bill in 1999, which consolidated the health insurance funds into one fund managed by the newly created National Health Insurance Corporation, a parastatal agency administered by the government.

The economy was hit especially hard by the Asian Financial Crisis. South Korea's chaebol firms were bailed out by the government to keep the economy afloat. Despite this, many companies were shuttered in the wake of the regional economic downturn. Unemployment skyrocketed, going from 2.6 percent in 1997 at the start of the financial crisis to 7 percent a year later in 1998. The percentage of those living below the poverty line also more than doubled, increasing from 3.9 percent in 1997 to 9.4 percent in 1999 (Shin, 2010). The halcyon days of uninterrupted economic growth ended abruptly. The effects of the regional financial crisis, combined with the electoral pressures inherent in democracy, forced political parties to consider deepening social welfare reform to both mitigate the crisis, and importantly, to win political support.

Soon after President Kim was elected, he established the tripartite council, bringing together industry, labor unions, and state officials to hammer out a new social and economic policy compact. Tripartite bargaining resulted in a landmark agreement in which the government relaxed regulations surrounding company layoffs. The tripartite bargain eased up and made more flexible the labor market. The trade-off for a more flexible and precarious labor market, however, was an agreement between the government and employers to cooperate and create more inclusive, ideally universal and redistributive, social insurance policies, including an announcement to establish a national pension scheme soon after (Peng and Wong, 2008). Like the earlier expansion and universalization of medical insurance during the late 1980s, the creation of the pension scheme reflected the political logic of winning electoral support through social policy reform.

The impact of democratic transition on social policy was also clear in Taiwan. During the late 1980s, when the KMT began liberalizing the political system, the incumbent government expanded coverage in its existing social insurance programs as well as created new ones. Specifically, the KMT expanded social insurance coverage in 1989, in addition to passing the youth welfare law, providing social protection benefits for children and family dependents. That same year, the government extended medical care insurance to farmers and other rural self-employed workers. For the first time, nonworking dependents were covered as well. These important reforms were then followed by the introduction of another health insurance scheme in 1990 designated for low-income households and financed primarily by the government (Ku, 1997).

Around this time, the KMT government created the cabinet-level Council for Labor Affairs (CLA), which spearheaded bureaucratic efforts to deepen Taiwan's welfare regime. The CLA was a key government proponent of stronger workplace regulations and social policy change. After a series of incremental reforms to the existing social insurance programs, the KMT government introduced unemployment benefits into the labor insurance scheme in 1999. This was an especially important policy change as the government for the first time allocated resources to unemployed workers, or those who earlier would have been considered economically "unproductive" and excluded from social insurance. The subsequent DPP government, which came into power in 2000, deepened, rather than scaled back, the KMT's earlier efforts to strengthen Taiwan's emerging welfare state. Notably, the DPP government legislated the Employment Insurance Act in 2003 and expanded unemployment benefits coverage even further to include part-time workers.

Similar to the South Korean experience, the most significant social policy reforms in democratizing Taiwan centered on the health care system. In 1988, one year after the KMT lifted Martial Law, the government publicly announced the formation of the national health insurance planning task force, signaling the KMT's commitment to deepen the welfare state. The government task force, made up of civil society allies, legislators from all parties and bureaucratic policymakers, designed the universal National Health Insurance (NHI) system over the next few years. The legislature passed the NHI Act in 1994 and implemented the program starting in 1995, on the eve of Taiwan's founding presidential elections a year later. As recounted in Wong's study *Healthy Democracies* (2004a), then President Lee Teng-Hui and the KMT's first presidential candidate implored the legislature to support and pass the NHI bill. Lee expected, rightly, that the introduction of a universal health insurance system would entail a significant political payoff to the incumbent regime from voters.

From a social welfare policy standpoint, the NHI reform was transformative. Unlike the fragmented medical insurance system initially introduced in South Korea and Japan, the NHI in Taiwan from the start was financed through an integrated (or "single pipe") financing mechanism, managed by the central Bureau of National Health Insurance. The integrated scheme maximized risk- and financial-pooling and encouraged redistribution. The NHI redistributed resources to ensure all citizens, and specifically the poor and nonworking dependents, benefited from the national health care system. After public protests erupted in 1995 against proposed co-pay rates, which activists claimed were too high, the government relented and drastically reduced out-of-pocket fee just before the NHI program went into effect. The adjustment appealed to poorer voters who feared the proposed copay rates might prevent them accessing the health system.

Right up to the eleventh hour, the imperative of winning electoral support shaped the development and implementation of social welfare policies in Taiwan (Wong, 2004a). The ruling party's electoral strategy depended on its willingness and capacity to respond to what voters sought. The KMT, like the

LDP in Japan much earlier on, positioned itself as an effective catch-all party, ideologically heterodox, inclusive, and attractive to a broad coalition of voters.

Taiwan's National Health Insurance program was – and remains – very popular among citizens. The government's financial and administrative contributions to the NHI from the start were significant, with direct public transfers to cover the health insurance premiums for self-employed workers and dependents (Lin Chenwei, 2018: 410). Public approval of the NHI was consistently over 95 percent during those early years. The electoral dividend for the KMT was huge, as the ruling party held up the NHI during its 1996 presidential campaign as evidence of the government's ability to engineer not just economic development, as it had in the past, but also sustained growth with equity through welfare state deepening.

2.3 Democracy's Impact

Democratic reform in South Korea and Taiwan during the late 1980s and 1990s coincided with significant social policy reforms and social welfare deepening (Wong, 2018; Chi and Kwon, 2012), just as it did in Japan during the postwar period of the 1950s. In all three cases, the introduction of democracy prompted the incumbent conservative governments to pursue social policy reform, expand existing social protection schemes, and create entirely new ones. Social policy reforms entailed the *universal* expansion of social welfare programs and a greater role for the governments in financing social protection. Notably in the heath sector in South Korea and Taiwan, social policy reforms resulted in more *redistributive* schemes as well, intended to benefit lower-income wage earners and their families. Benefits for dependents and the unemployed reflected a significant move away from the narrower, productivist logic that had shaped social policy reform during the postwar developmental state era.

But while the coincidence of democratic reform and social welfare deepening is clear, *how* democratization affected social policy reform requires further explication (Shim, 2019; Wong, 2005). The remainder of this section explores the impact the introduction of democracy in East Asia had on the direction and scope social policy reform, prompting a significant shift from earlier commitments to productivism and economic growth to later deepening the welfare state.

2.3.1 Electoral Imperatives

Public opinion about the idea of economic development evolved and changed in democratic South Korea and Taiwan during the 1990s, as it did in Japan in the 1950s. During the early postwar period, when East Asia's economies were poor and reeling in the aftermath of the war and waning days of colonialism, "development" was essentially – and understandably – synonymous with economic growth. However, the ways in which citizens and policymakers view the idea of economic development evolved. With the introduction of democracy, first in Japan and later in South Korea and Taiwan, the concept of development came to include other priorities such as achieving more socioeconomic equity, fostering redistribution, and the fulfilment social and democratic citizenship.

The Japanese case is instructive. Deborah Milly's important study (1999), *Poverty, Equality and Growth*, chronicles how political competition during the late 1940s and into the 1950s between the Japanese Socialist Party (JSP) and the conservative parties contributed to a shift among Japanese voters and their views about the role that government ought to play in social welfare. With electoral pressure coming initially from the JSP, the conservative LDP government was compelled to pursue an electoral "accommodation" strategy, as Milly puts it, and to integrate social policy reform into its electoral platform. As argued previously, the conservative parties' shift to the center reflected an electoral strategy to address both the fact of growing socioeconomic inequality as well as changing public attitudes and voters' preferences regarding the government's role in mitigating such inequality. Voters' ideas about and preferences for more robust welfare states affected how Japan's conservative parties evolved with democracy.

During the 1990s, South Korean public opinion data reveal similarly changing views about the relationship between development, inequality and the state. In a 1992 survey, for instance, nearly two-thirds of respondents felt the widening income gap in Korean society needed to be addressed. Citizens also believed that workers should have greater influence when it came to government policy decision-making. A majority of survey respondents, for instance, agreed that "failure of government policies is one reason for poverty" in South Korea, putting the blame on the state for rising inequality (Wong, 2004a: 135–136). In a 1998 survey soon after the Asian Financial Crisis an even larger majority – over 80 percent – of South Koreans believed the state ought to take on the responsibility for social welfare provision (Shin and Rose, 1998: 35). Political parties needed to account for evolving voter preferences as they competed for political power, and voters in South Korea increasingly felt the government needed to take on a larger role in fostering more balanced economic development.

Attitudes among citizens and voters in democratizing Taiwan reflected a similarly evolving sentiment. Public opinion during the 1990s, when Taiwan was amid its democratic transition, captured this shift away from a focus on economic growth alone to more robust, government-administered social safety nets. According to a 1991 survey, for instance, only 28 percent of respondents in Taiwan expressed satisfaction with the government's commitment to social welfare, while 44 percent were dissatisfied. Not surprisingly, nearly 70 percent of respondents felt that government spending for social welfare programs was too low and needed to increase. Meanwhile, less than 1 percent of those surveyed believed government spending for social policy was too high, and only 0.4 percent felt that it should decrease. In 1994, the percentage of respondents dissatisfied with Taiwan's social welfare regime increased to 50 percent (Wong, 2004a: 135–136).

Like in South Korea, Taiwanese citizens, who had benefited from decades of sustained economic growth, wanted a more, not less, interventionist welfare state. Not only were citizens increasingly aware of, and dissatisfied with, rising inequality in South Korea and Taiwan, voters believed it was the government's responsibility, and not the individual or their family, to provide social protection. Expectations of what government *should do* and *can do* transformed during the period of democratic transition. Chung-In Moon observes that in South Korea the "developmentalist ideology couched in terms of growth and security has been devalued," and citizen "demands for re-distribution, welfare, quality of life and environmental integrity constitute new political and ideological mandates" (Moon, 1999: 9). The postwar focus solely on growth and economic productivity was no longer acceptable to voters. The productivist priority of the developmental state had given way to a more inclusive notion of development.

From an electoral point of view, evolving voters' preferences pointed the way to a winning electoral formula. In Japan, as we saw in Section 1, changing public opinion about the desirability of the welfare state combined with voter preferences expressed at the ballot box prompted the conservative LDP to coopt the socialist's progressive social policy reform agendas and position itself as a catch-all political party. Prime Minister Ikeda, whose LDP government was elected with a strong majority in 1960, was described as a "pragmatic politician" who "employed a centrist political strategy, combined with accommodation toward labor and the left in the form of moderate social policies" (Milly, 1999).

The introduction of democratic elections in South Korea and Taiwan in the 1990s similarly prompted the incumbent conservative ruling parties to legislate and implement significant social policy reforms in health, old-age income security, unemployment protection as well as benefits for dependents. In the run-up to the 1993 local elections in Taiwan opposition DPP candidates floated the idea of a universal pension program in their campaign. The incumbent KMT candidates countered, not by rebuffing the DPP's proposal, but instead by doubling-down on their promise, committing to expand, not retrench, the government's old-age benefits scheme and increase the size of the pension benefit if elected. As Ku Yeun-Wen recounts, because of the 1993 local election, "pensions became a big issue all over the island and the size of the allowance [benefit] grew and grew" (Ku, 1997: 249). Debate between local candidates during the 1993 campaign escalated their respective social policy promises.

This pattern of electoral competition and the *ratcheting-up* of social policy pledges continued into the 2000s in democratic Taiwan. Soon after the DPP government took power in 2000, the newly elected ruling party expanded the unemployment insurance reforms that had been introduced by the KMT a few years earlier, when it passed landmark labor protection legislation in 2003. Likewise, in the run-up to South Korea's first legislative elections in 1988, the incumbent DJP government expanded medical insurance to key electoral constituencies in the countryside and again one year later to urban workers. Conservative governments later on did the same, increasing the state's role in providing social protection.

In democratic East Asia, electoral incentives ensured that social welfare reform became a prominent issue in democratic contests. The introduction of competitive multiparty elections and the imperative to win a broad base of voter support incentivized parties to pursue social policy reform as a key plank in their platform.

2.3.2 Ideological Flexibility

What is particularly striking about the politics of welfare state deepening in East Asia is that reform occurred in the absence of an electorally dominant leftist political party. Welfare state deepening was not championed by elected left-leaning socialist governments, as expected by conventional theories of the welfare state. Initial efforts to deepen the welfare state in Japan, South Korea, and Taiwan were instead led by historically conservative incumbent parties.

In Japan, the Socialist Party was a viable political party only during the very early days of postwar democracy. The JSP was quickly sidelined, as descried earlier in this Element, giving way to nearly four decades of LDP electoral dominance. In democratizing South Korea, the main opposition parties led by Kim Young-Sam and Kim Dae-Jung, though nominally progressive owing to their opposition status, nonetheless drew their electoral support from their charismatic leaders and regional bases of support rather than any strong ideological commitment to social welfare policies. Meanwhile, the opposition DPP in Taiwan was founded as an ethnic Taiwanese party and emerged initially to exploit the ethnic cleavages dividing Taiwanese society. While some factions within it leaned toward a more social democratic policy agenda, the DPP was hardly a leftist political party (Shim, 2020).

In none of the three cases did a labor-backed, social democratic party of the European kind become an enduring governing party. Leftist governments did not drive welfare state development in democratic East Asia. Yet, power resources theories of the welfare state contend that strong leftist parties are a precondition to more progressive social welfare policies and programs. Power resources theories of the welfare state thus find it unlikely that social policy regimes could expand to become universal and redistributive without strong leftist parties in power. However, and counterintuitively, in democratizing Japan, South Korea, and Taiwan, it was the *absence*, rather than the presence, of strong leftist political parties that contributed to the deepening of the welfare state.

Ideological flexibility in terms of the left–right cleavage rather than ideological rigidity created the conditions under which conservative political parties could embrace social policy reform platforms to attract voters. The left–right ideological cleavage was never deeply entrenched in the political party system, especially in South Korea and Taiwan, and only for a very brief while in postwar Japan. The absence of the left, and the absence of a left–right ideological cleavage more generally, meant the political party system was ideologically flexible. The absence of strong leftist parties opened up the ideological space for nominally and historically conservative ones to credibly coopt progressive social democratic reform agendas (Shim, 2020; Wong, 2004b). Because of this, conservative parties such as the LDP, the DJP, and the KMT were able to strategically shift their electoral appeals leftwards and toward the center without betraying any ideological commitment or alienating their traditional voter base. They gradually embraced a social welfare reform agenda without being politically penalized.

In South Korea, recall, it was the conservative incumbent DJP that initially and rapidly expanded social welfare benefits during the late 1980s to secure voter support. In Taiwan, the KMT ratcheted up its social policy reform commitments in a "race to the top" in welfare reform, rather than retrench the government's role in social protection when it faced competition from the opposition DPP. Likewise, the LDP in Japan introduced universal social insurance schemes in health and pensions throughout the 1960s, as they proved to be a winning formula in elections. Importantly, ideological flexibility in the party system not only *permitted* incumbent ruling parties to occupy what political scientists refer to as "issue space" in electoral competition, the absence of the left–right cleavage in the party system *incentivized* otherwise nominally conservative parties to campaign on popular social welfare reform platforms (Wong, 2004a).

2.3.3 The Legacies of Equitable Growth

One of the distinctive characteristics of postwar East Asian development was its experience of growth with equity, which was described in Section 1 of this Element. The developmental state in Japan, South Korea, and Taiwan fostered rapid economic growth and industrialization, while maintaining a relatively egalitarian distribution of income. Growth with equity mitigated class conflict and obviated the pressing need for redistributive social welfare programs during the period of rapid economic development. Furthermore, growth with equity had a profound effect on how the democratizing governments, specifically in South Korea and Taiwan, deepened their role in expanding their social welfare regimes.

The legacy of equitable growth is one that narrowed the income gap between the haves and have-nots, reinforcing the *perception* of relative egalitarianism among citizens. Extensive survey data shows the vast majority of people in Japan, South Korea, and Taiwan believed that they were part of the middle class (Hsiao, 1999). Most people perceived themselves to neither be excessively wealthy nor be poor, but rather part of the large middle strata of society. Indeed, relatively good wages, full employment combined with strong (and even government-subsidized) labor markets, state investment in education, and labor market upskilling and upward social mobility gave most people the sense that they belonged to the middle class. What failed to emerge in developmental East Asia, therefore, was a distinctive and mobilized working-class consciousness, such as what power resource theorists of the welfare state might predict should happen in rapidly industrializing societies.

Growth with equity – and importantly, the enduring perception of equitable growth – lowered the costs of implementing redistributive social welfare policies in three ways. First, equitable growth narrowed the economic distance between the rich and poor, and thus mitigated the *economic costs* of redistribution across social classes. Put another way, the redistribution of resources (be it income, public resources, health, and so on) through social policy did not have to traverse as large a distance in what were relatively egalitarian economies. Second, growth with equity similarly reduced the *social costs* of redistribution. Because class distinctions were not as conspicuous nor entrenched socially in East Asia, the perceived social distance between the have and have-nots was narrower in Japan, South Korea, and Taiwan. The blurring of social classes thus made redistributive social welfare reform more acceptable to society broadly (Wong, 2019).

Third, rapid, yet equitable, economic growth reduced the *political costs* of socioeconomic redistribution. Growth with equity stunted the development of a strong political left in South Korea and Taiwan, which also softened the left–right ideological cleavage in democratic politics, as described previously. Opposition parties by and large mobilized voters along regional (in South Korea) or ethnic lines (Taiwan), as well as on a pro-democracy regime cleavage, rather than along class lines. The absence of a strong leftist party in democratizing South Korea and Taiwan thus created the political space for the incumbent ruling parties to position themselves as centrist, catch-all parties. The political cost to the DJP and KMT to campaign on a social welfare reform agenda was negligible, in that voters did not punish them for coopting progressive social welfare reform agendas into their electoral platforms (Wong, 2019).

2.3.4 Additive Reform

Democratic politicians and policymakers in Japan, South Korea, and Taiwan not only needed to *promise* social policy reforms to win elections, ultimately they had to *deliver* social policy reform to voters if they expected to hold onto political power. Policymakers' promises for reform needed to not only appeal to voters' preferences, but they also had to be credible in their ability to implement their promised reforms. In other words, they required easy pathways to achieve their social welfare promises.

Policymakers pursued what Peng and Wong refer to as "additive reform" (Peng and Wong, 2008); that is, social policymakers deepened the welfare state through the *addition* of social insurance funds and by expanding social protection benefits, but *without any structural reform* to the preexisting social welfare regime. Policymakers deepened the welfare state not by dismantling existing schemes and re-constructing social protection systems anew, but rather by building upon and expanding the social insurance model. Importantly, none of the emerging social welfare regimes in democratic East Asia resembled the government-financed Nordic welfare states. Radical structural reform was not a viable political option for social policymakers.

For example, Japan's LDP government achieved universal health insurance by expanding coverage to existing medical insurance funds and by adding new ones. Structurally, the preexisting social insurance system remained intact. Similarly in South Korea, the universalization of medical insurance during the late 1980s was achieved by adding new insurance funds for urban and rural self-employed workers, while maintaining the overall insurance structure of the system. The expansion of Korea's pension system adhered to the same process, with the addition of new old-age income security schemes to the existing social insurance system. In these examples, additive reform, rather than structural renovation, offered the path of least resistance. The implementation of the 1995 National Health Insurance (NHI) system in Taiwan required arguably the most extensive structural reform with the creation of a single-pipe insurance system. However, the NHI remained a social insurance scheme, dependent on worker and employer (and some government) insurance contributions. The introduction of universal and redistributive health insurance did not entail a more radical transformation to a solely government-financed universal medicare system. In none of the three cases did we see social welfare deepening involve a structural move away from the social insurance model, which had been introduced in Japan, South Korea, and Taiwan well before they were universalized.

Additive reform of the existing social insurance regimes lowered the political and institutional costs of policy expansion. To be sure, institutional path dependency made it more difficult for policymakers to alter the existing social insurance structure (see Kwon, 2008). Politically speaking, politicians, especially conservative incumbents, needed social policy wins, and turned to reforms that were not only popular among voters, but which could be implemented quickly and with little risk and cost.

And yet, additive reform, despite being "easier" to achieve and more viable for policymakers, was nonetheless significant in terms of its socioeconomic impact. As Peng and Wong (2008) argue, institutional continuity "in form" does not necessarily mean continuity in "institutional purpose." Despite adding onto existing social insurance institutions, the reforms that were introduced in democratizing East Asia were transformative. They universalized coverage, increased redistribution, resulted in more fiscal contributions from the government, and, most importantly, reflected a fundamental shift in the purpose of the social insurance model, away from the productivist ethos of the postwar period toward social protection for even the most vulnerable and economically unproductive. Simply put, additive reform transformed the welfare state's *institutional purpose*.

2.3.5 Mainstreaming Welfare

The coincidence of democratization and welfare state deepening in East Asia countered global trends in social welfare policy reform. Welfare regimes around the world were retrenching their social policy commitments during the 1990s, precisely the time when democratizing South Korea and Taiwan were expanding theirs. What is especially remarkable about the East Asian experience was the extent to which the idea of social welfare became increasingly central to *mainstream politics*, when in many other countries the welfare state was becoming fiscally strained and progressive social policy agendas increasingly marginalized.

As this section asserts, in democratizing East Asia – first in Japan during the 1950s and later in South Korea and Taiwan during the 1990s – citizens and voters increasingly demanded more, not less, social protection. From a normative point of view, voters believed the governments in Japan, South Korea, and Taiwan needed to play a more significant role in addressing fairness in the economy and society more generally. In terms of voter preferences and public opinion, citizens wanted more welfare statism, not less. Universal and redistributive social welfare reform was not a policy agenda that could be pushed to the margins of mainstream democratic debate. Political parties and politicians, even historically conservative ones, ratcheted up, rather than go back on, their social policy commitments. They mainstreamed welfare.

3 Adaptation for the Twenty-First Century

3.1 The Welfare State in Post-Industrial East Asia

The governments in Japan, South Korea, and Taiwan continued to reform and deepen their commitments to the welfare state throughout the 1990s and into the 2000s. Government spending on social policy programs grew considerably during this period. Between 1990 and 2000, social spending increased by almost 50 percent in Japan, growing from 11.1 percent of GDP to close to 16.3 percent. Meanwhile, social policy expenditures nearly doubled in South Korea and Taiwan during the same period, increasing from 5.2 percent of GDP to 9 percent in the former, and from 6.8 percent to over 13 percent in the latter (OECD; Lindert, 2004; Chan, 2008).

Democratically elected governments created new social policy programs throughout the 1990s and 2000s as well. In the wake of the Asian Financial Crisis, the Kim Dae-Jung administration in South Korea implemented a national pension scheme, reviving a policy proposal which had been introduced earlier but was shelved. A decade later, well into the 2000s, the conservative Kim Myung-Bak government introduced a raft of Keynesian policy interventions to soften the blow of economic downturns (Yang, 2012). South Korea was not alone in social policy innovation. In Taiwan, KMT and DPP governments introduced new social protection programs aimed specifically at vulnerable workers and their families. Governing parties, both KMT and DPP, in Taiwan also continued to expand the scope and generosity of the decades-old Labor Insurance program throughout the 1990s and 2000s.

Importantly, both nominally conservative and progressive governments in Japan, South Korea, and Taiwan remained committed to the social policy reform agenda that had been established during the period of democratization. Not unlike in Japan, where earlier the conservative LDP embraced a more inclusive approach to economic development, becoming a catch-all party and essentially coopting the socialist's progressive reform agenda, conservative ruling parties in South Korea and Taiwan embraced social policy reform to win votes. Social policy reform, as argued in the previous section of this Element, proved to be an enduring, winning policy agenda for contending political parties in democratic East Asia.

Despite government commitments to deepen the welfare state, the social policy regimes in Japan, South Korea, and Taiwan nonetheless confronted a new wave of political and economic pressures associated with *post-industrial* economic development during the 1990s and 2000s. It was not smooth sailing for these emerging welfare states, as it was not for many social policy regimes around the world. These new pressures have had a significant effect on the evolution of the welfare state over the past few decades. Specifically, the strong state regimes in East Asia that formerly and ably guided economic development in the postwar period were forced to retreat. Liberalizing economic reforms eroded their state capacity to lead economic development, including in the area of social welfare reform. Formerly strong states are no longer as autonomous or capable. Moreover, new risks associated with post-industrialism, new vulnerabilities among workers, and new sources of welfare state exclusion and stratification emerged during the 1990s and 2000s. A significant decline in manufacturing employment, for instance, fundamentally transformed the structure of labor markets in the region, which had been the backbone of the postwar welfare regimes in East Asia. Meanwhile, the rapid rise in informal work and precarious employment created additional pressures on the welfare state.

This section examines how the current political economic context, shaped by post-industrial pressures and labor market transformations, has forced East Asia's welfare regimes to adapt in significant ways. Social welfare policy has emphasized employment and work in increasingly flexibilized labor markets, rather than policies aimed at redistribution. Furthermore, social policy reform in recent years has tended to focus on specific vulnerable segments within society, rather than the entire population, the latter being the hallmark of welfare state universalism. Welfare state deepening that occurred during the 1990s, including the expansion of many social protection schemes discussed in the previous section, has given way to more targeted social programs. The challenges associated with post-industrialism are not unique to East Asia, however, and the deployment of labor market interventions as a social policy tool has become the norm in social policy reform worldwide, a point that will be taken up in the concluding section (Fleckenstein and Lee, 2017; Emmenegger et al., 2012).

3.2 New Political Economic Context

The postwar developmental state described earlier in this Element was fit for purpose and for its time. Beginning in the 1990s and into the 2000s, however, the democratic developmental state had run its course in terms of its capacity and ability to effectively allocate state resources to achieve its goals. New competitive pressures, including the need to climb increasingly complicated global value chains, have required states to loosen their grip on the industrial policy levers that worked so effectively in the past.

3.2.1 The Decline of the Developmental State

In Japan, signs of the retreating developmental state model emerged as early as the 1980s. One of the key policy instruments the Japanese developmental state used to create and support industrial winners was its manipulation of exchange rate policies, specifically by competitively devaluing its currency to Japanese exports cheaper. The Plaza Accords, initiated by the United States in 1985, forced Japan to revalue the yen, undermining its trade advantages. The accords signaled the growing intolerance of the global economy toward market interventions by the Japanese state, reflecting international pressure on East Asia's developmental states to play by the same rules as others.

South Korea and Taiwan initially benefited from the effects of the 1985 Plaza Accords. They capitalized on Japan's adjustment and rapidly grew their market share in manufacturing exports, especially in the electronics manufacturing sector. However, their competitive advantage proved ephemeral, as all three economies soon faced increasingly stiff competition from Southeast Asia and China as these later developers grew their own manufacturing industries. Japan, South Korea, and Taiwan were forced to offshore their sunset industries in search of cheaper skilled labor. In turn, they needed to develop new competitive strengths in sunrise, high-tech sectors, such as advanced electronics and information technologies, software, and life sciences innovation and biotechnology (Wong, 2006).

Japan was already well invested at the time in the development of new cutting-edge technology industries, having been the lead economy in the region for decades. South Korea and Taiwan, on the other hand, were only beginning their transition to becoming R&D-intensive innovation economies (Wong, 2011). Whereas in the past, the East Asian developmental state was effective in developing their manufacturing industries through centralized mechanisms to reverse-engineer and essentially copy technologies that had been developed elsewhere, the imperatives of first-order innovation eluded such top-down directives (Wong, 2011). To be competitive in emerging lucrative post-industrial industries, the governments in Japan, South Korea, and Taiwan needed to liberalize their economies, not further centralize political economic authority. The state's earlier approach to industrial upgrading had run its course in the face of the highly uncertain, post-industrial, innovation economy. Its continued effectiveness in delivering development was questioned.

The developmental state model suffered a more existential blow when Japan's economic bubble burst in the early 1990s, portending crisis more generally in the region. Japan's economic crisis revealed an inflated asset market and a history of profligate nonperforming industrial loans. The economy stalled and only gradually recovered over the next several decades. Its setback in the early 1990s set the stage for the more widespread economic turmoil in the region, culminating in the Asian Financial Crisis of 1997 (Pempel, 1999). The Japanese crisis brought into question the ability of the developmental states to continue to direct economic growth from the top-down.

The 1997 financial crisis hit South Korea especially hard. Decades of easy access to government credit supported by industrial policies directed at underwriting massive chaebol firms left Korean industries vulnerable. As other economies in the region collapsed and set off a chain reaction, and as creditors started to call in their debts, the South Korean economy reeled. The value of the *Won* plummeted, forcing the Korean government to defend its currency against predatory speculators. Meanwhile, exports, which had been the lifeblood of the economy, declined. Damaged corporate assets and the spread of nonperforming loans in South Korea meant that many once-formidable manufacturing firms were forced to shutter their factories. Critics pointed to the cozy and even corrupt relationships between state officials and South Korea's industrial giants, highlighting the structural problems associated with tight government–business relations and bloated firms that were too big to fail.

In other words, the developmental state, once lauded for its role in modernizing and industrializing East Asia's economies, was seen to be the problem and not the solution to the region's economic woes. The end of the state-led economic development era loomed on the horizon, and with it the end of the strong state apparatus that had once been so central to East Asia's postwar dynamism, including the emergence of the East Asian welfare state. The decline of the developmental state during this era foreshadowed the waning ability and willingness of East Asian governments to stay the welfare state course.

3.2.2 Labor Market Transformation

The economies of Japan, South Korea, and Taiwan experienced additional strains due to significant structural economic transformations during the

1990s and 2000s, specifically with respect to their domestic labor markets. As the three economies shifted into new post-industrial, tertiary sectors, the shape of the labor market changed as well. Manufacturing employment declined rapidly in the region after the 1990s. In South Korea, manufacturing jobs as a share of total employment declined from 27.2 percent in 1990 to just 17 percent by 2015 (Asian Development Bank, 2020). Meanwhile, employment in service and tertiary industries reached nearly 70 percent of the labor market in Japan, South Korea, and Taiwan by 2015.

Labor union density, which was already quite low in the region compared with other industrialized economies, declined rapidly as more and more workers sought employment outside of manufacturing sectors. Union membership in Japan, shrunk from 25 percent of the workforce to around 17 percent between 1990 and 2015 (Watanabe, 2018; Gottfried, 2014). In South Korea, the decline in union membership was even more stark as union membership rates decreased from 18.4 percent 1990 to just 10.3 percent in 2005 (Lee and Chung, 2008). What were once industrial manufacturing economies had become predominantly tertiary ones. As a result, labor markets became more flexible and precarious.

As the structure of the industrial economy and labor markets began to change during the 1990s and 2000s, unemployment rates started to rise as well, adding more pressure on the social welfare regimes. Gone were the days of full employment as the de facto social safety net, or what Fleckenstein and Lee characterize as "welfare through work" (2017: 38). In Taiwan and South Korea, unemployment rates more than doubled during the 1990s and into the 2000s. In South Korea specifically, the unemployment rate nearly tripled from 2.6 percent to 7 percent in the one year after the financial crisis.

Governments needed to respond. After Japan's economy went into a recession beginning in the early 1990s, the government adapted by amending labor regulations to make it easier for companies to dismiss and lay off workers. This was a concession to the national federations of employers' associations, which demanded more flexibility in how they managed their workforce. Notably, these new employment laws permitted companies to hire "discretionary workers" on short-term contracts (Watanabe, 2018: 586; Gottfried, 2014; Peng, 2012). New regulations and laws severely undermined the lifetime employment compact between companies and workers that had mediated management–labor tensions for decades. The labor market shift also eroded the company-based welfare system that was the foundation of Japan's social welfare regime, as fewer workers were able to access company social protection schemes.

The 1997 Asian Financial Crisis prompted the South Korean government to find ways to accommodate the concerns and interests of employers, workers and labor organizations, as well as government policymakers. As noted in Section 2, the tripartite committee agreed upon several new social policy innovations, including the expansion and integration of the medical insurance system. However, social policy advances were traded off with regulatory changes that eased restrictions on firms to lay off workers (Lee, 2011; see also Shin, 2010). Like in Japan, the beneficiaries of South Korea's company-based welfare regime were not spared in the shift toward a more flexible labor market.

While Taiwan was somewhat inoculated from the severity of the effects of the financial crisis because of the predominance of SMEs in Taiwan's industrial economy, domestic companies, and specifically manufacturing firms that faced increased competition from China and other late developing economies, were not immune to cost-cutting imperatives. Beginning in the 1990s, Taiwanese firms had to increasingly rely on flexible, informal arrangements with workers. Employers hired more "dispatched" or temporary workers on short-term contracts (Hsiao, 2013; Lee, 2011).

The flexibilization of the labor market contributed to a rapid change in employment patterns. Formal sectors jobs have been replaced with part-time, nonformal or nonstandard forms of employment. The dualization of the labor market – the distinction between formal and nonformal employment – is not unique to Asia, but, rather, increasingly experienced in all post-industrial societies. As defined by the International Labor Organization, nonformal work is part-time, limited term contractual, unregulated, temporary or informal sector work. Advanced post-industrial economies over the past few decades have experienced the decline in employment in traditional manufacturing industries and rapid growth in tertiary and service sector work, much of it found in informal employment arrangements.

In Japan, in 2010, over 28 percent of workers were employed in "non-standard employment arrangements" (Gottfried, 2014: 269). According to labor market surveys, the percentage of workers employed in nonstandard work more than doubled between the mid-1980s and 2010, increasing from 15 percent to over 34 percent (cited in Tanaka, 2019: 20; see also Kezier, 2008). In South Korea, the nonstandard or nonformal employment rate dramatically increased throughout the 1990s, cresting at 55.7 percent of the workforce in 2001. South Korea ranked among the highest in the OECD in terms of temporarily employed workers as a share of the total labor force in 2007 (Lee, 2011: 249). The rate of nonstandard employment declined during the first decade of the 2000s but remained around 50 percent in 2012 (Cho and Choi, 2017: 599–600).

The size of the nonstandard labor market in Taiwan is considerably smaller than in South Korea and Japan. Government figures from Taiwan report the proportion of workers employed part-time, on short-term contracts, or considered "dispatched" temporary workers was just 8.8 percent of the workforce in 2010. This relatively low figure reflects the SME-dominant nature of the economy, in which a large proportion of workers are self-employed or are small-scale entrepreneurs for whom labor market mobility is common. Sophia Lee (2016) contends that Taiwan's distinctive industrial structure and fluid labor market have mitigated somewhat the stratifying effects of dualized employment arrangements. Nonetheless, the size of the nonstandard labor market in Taiwan increased alarmingly fast, nearly quadrupling from just 2.4 percent of the workforce to just under 9 percent from 2001 to 2010. Analysts attribute the rapid growth in nonstandard or temporary work to government efforts to relax labor regulations during the late 1990s and 2000s (Hsiao, 2013: 378–380; Shi, 2012). Taiwan's labor market adjustments mirror, though to a smaller degree, the labor market regulatory reforms in South Korea and Japan.

Labor market dualization, and specifically the sharp increase in nonstandard work arrangements, have created new configurations of winners and losers in the economy, exacerbating existing as well as creating new cleavages. In general, nonstandard workers enjoy considerably less employment security and experience more uncertainty when it comes to income stability. Nonstandard and informal sector workers are also compensated considerably less than their full-time formal sector counterparts. According to the OECD, nonstandard workers earn between just 40 percent and 60 percent of formally employed worker's wages for the same work. Furthermore, less-educated workers account for a disproportionate share of nonstandard employees, between three and four times that of higher-educated (i.e. university-educated) workers in South Korea and Taiwan. Less-educated, nonstandard workers, which make up an increasingly large share of the post-industrial workforce in East Asia, are poorer than their counterparts in the formal labor market (Hsiao, 2013; Shi, 2012; Lee, 2011).

Importantly, labor market dualization and worker stratification have not cleaved solely along class lines. The growth in informal and nonstandard employment has disproportionately impacted women and young people in East Asia. In South Korea, for example, women are 1.5 times more likely to be employed in a nonstandard or part-time work arrangement. Even more starkly in Japan, women are three times more likely to be informally employed than men. From the 1980s to the 2000s, the nonstandard employment rate among Japanese women increased from around 30 percent to over 50 percent. By 2007, women accounted for over 70 percent of all part-time or nonstandard workers in Japan (Gottfried, 2014; Lee, 2011).

The negative effects of labor market dualization are more acutely experienced not just among women, but also by specific demographic age groups. Just as women are more likely to be employed in nonstandard work arrangements in East Asia, so too are younger people. Though the growth of nonstandard employment has been experienced across all age groups, the growth rate has been fastest among young workers. In Japan, for instance, the share of younger workers (less than twenty-four years old) employed in nonstandard work doubled from the 1990s to the first decade of the 2000s. Similarly in Taiwan, workers under the age of twenty-four accounted for the largest cohort of workers employed part-time or in temporary work arrangements in 2010 (Shi, 2012: 86).

Older workers, like their younger counterparts, are vulnerable as well, especially as their prospects for labor market re-entry (when unemployed) are especially dim. In 2008, older (over fifty-five years old) workers in South Korea accounted for more than half of all those employed in nonstandard work. Similar rates of informal employment among older workers are evident in Japan. In Taiwan, older workers are more likely to be informally employed than other age groups, though to a lesser extent compared to other East Asian societies given the high labor mobility rates in the SME-dominant economy (Lee, 2011).

Informal sector workers are disadvantaged in many ways. Due to their precarious labor market status, nonstandard workers are largely excluded from social welfare regimes. Because East Asia's welfare programs are occupationally based or predominantly company-based welfare schemes, those working in nonstandard employment arrangements are often unable to claim benefits from their employers. Informally employed workers are also less able to access labor dispute mechanisms, legal recourse or restitution, thus leaving them vulnerable to workplace injuries, accidents and other abuses (Shizume, Kato, and Matsuda, 2021; Kim, 2017).

3.2.3 Insiders and Outsiders

Owing to their precarious employment arrangements, nonstandard employees and informal sector workers are often marginalized and excluded from social insurance schemes mandated by the government. Stratification and exclusion from social protection is evident in post-industrial East Asia and elsewhere; these problems are not distinctive in Japan, South Korea, and Taiwan. David Rueda (2008), in his study of European social democracies, observes that in post-industrial societies the division between labor market "insiders" (i.e. formally employed) and "outsiders" (nonstandard workers) has stratified social welfare policy beneficiaries into what he calls, correspondingly, welfare state insiders and outsiders. The dualization of the labor market in post-industrial

Europe, similar to East Asia, has resulted in the *dualization of social welfare regimes*, which protect some while excluding others.

Exclusion from social insurance benefits among nonstandard workers is particularly striking in South Korea and Japan, where the share of nonstandard work increased most dramatically, and where most formal workers are protected in company-based insurance schemes (Tanaka, 2019; Kim, 2017). In South Korea, 98 percent of formally employed full-time workers benefited from the Korean pension program in 2010, though less than one-third of nonstandard workers were covered under any old-age income security scheme. Likewise, nearly 99 percent of standard, full-time workers were covered by Korea's medical insurance program, whereas just 36 percent of nonstandard workers enjoyed access to the program. In Japan, the situation for nonstandard workers is only slightly better. In 2010, for instance, 99.5 percent of standard, full-time Japanese workers could claim pension and health benefits from their employer, while about half of those employed in nonstandard work were covered by any social insurance scheme. In Japan, firms are not required to contribute to social insurance benefits for part-time or nonstandard workers (Cho and Choi, 2017: 601; see also Yang, 2013; Shin, 2010; Kim, 2016). In both countries, foreign temporary workers are excluded from social protection as well.

Stratification in social insurance regimes in Japan, South Korea, and Taiwan is not new. As argued in Section 1, occupationally and company-based social insurance benefits provided by firms to their employees have historically been more generous for formal sector employees than other kinds of nonstandard workers. As emphasized throughout this Element, East Asian social insurance programs were always tied with one's work, and the benefits from social insurance were stratified along workers' employment status. The rapid rise in unemployment and the marginalization of nonstandard workers have exacerbated the distinction between the haves and have-nots. The dualization of the labor market in post-industrial East Asia widened existing gaps in the social safety net.

According to Rueda, the post-industrial economy not only exacerbates and exposes new social risks, but the rapidly changing structure of the labor market also reveals a new political economy of social welfare reform. The conventional model of welfare state expansion, which reflects a specific and earlier mode of industrial capitalism, depended on the relative power and political resources available to mobilize *formal sector workers*, and not informal ones, Power resources theory, notably, focuses on the ability of industrial workers to politically organize, and with one political voice in consolidated trade unions, to pressure democratic governments to implement more generous welfare programs. Industrial workers, it is assumed, share a common interest in welfare state expansion. In this theory, formal sector workers' preferences are presumed to be aligned.

But what about informal workers? Rueda's theory of welfare state insiders and outsiders contends that labor market insiders have different social policy preferences than outsiders. According to Rueda, workers, broadly defined, are not unified but are differentiated and stratified according to their labor market status: insider or outsider. Whereas unionized formal sector workers (insiders) are primarily concerned with collectively mobilizing for higher wages and employment benefits, informal workers (outsiders) prefer government policy interventions that activate the labor market and create more employment opportunities. Simply put, insiders and outsiders' interests are not aligned; they have diametrically opposed preferences. Furthermore, labor market outsiders are less capable in politically mobilizing their rank-and-file and thus exert less political pressure, be it in their ability to lobby the government or influence policies through the ballot box (Garay, 2017). Outsiders are not only excluded from the welfare state, but marginalized in the political arena as well.

In East Asia's post-industrial economy, therefore, the most vulnerable and in need of social protection are workers who are employed in the increasingly sizable informal labor market; they are, in Rueda's language, labor market and welfare state outsiders. Vulnerable workers in Japan, South Korea, and Taiwan are those without long-term contracts and ineligible for the benefits that come with such arrangements. As labor market outsiders, informal sector workers are likely to be paid less, more vulnerable to unemployment, and, importantly, less capable in mobilizing politically. They are the most vulnerable, yet also the weakest politically.

3.3 East Asian Post-Industrial Welfare Regimes

East Asian governments have responded to the challenges of labor market dualization, the challenges of insiders, outsiders, and social policy reform in two ways. These are discussed further below. First, without abandoning their commitments to providing and administering social insurance protection to formal sector workers, the post-industrial welfare regimes in Japan, South Korea, and Taiwan have also increasingly focused on *reforming labor market policies*. As Rueda (2008) and others expect, to create employment opportunities for precarious workers requires governments to introduce passive and active labor market policies to stabilize otherwise precarious work for labor market outsiders.

Second, East Asia's post-industrial welfare regimes have also increasingly *targeted* specific segments of the population, particularly those who are especially vulnerable to labor market precariousness. Social policies implemented during the 2000s have notably explicitly targeted impoverished households and individuals, older people who require long-term care and other social services, and women who have been forced to exit the labor market to care for elderly members of the household and their children. Targeted social welfare policies mark a significant shift in East Asia's social welfare regimes. They reflect, I contend, a deliberate move away from universalist social programs, which were characterized by the reforms of the 1990s, toward a patchwork of targeted social protection schemes.

3.3.1 Labor Market Adjustments

Liberalizing labor market reforms after the 1997 Asian Financial Crisis signaled the South Korean government's waning commitment to a full employment strategy, when it allowed firms to lay off workers in the wake of the financial crisis. The result was the flexibilization of the labor market, the creation of precariously employed outsiders. Workers who had come to expect stable and even life-long employment suddenly confronted the possibility of being laid off, and many were. To accommodate workers, however, the government integrated the medical insurance program, making it more generous for all citizens. Beyond that, the government looked to plug other holes in the social safety net created by the new flexible labor regulations. Notably, it expanded the scope of coverage in the employment insurance program to provide an income safety net for workers employed in smaller firms and who found themselves unemployed (Yang, 2012).

The other East Asian governments followed suit, adjusting their unemployment schemes to support vulnerable workers. In 2001, for instance, the Japanese government expanded coverage in company employment insurance schemes to include part-time workers. The government in Taiwan introduced unemployment benefits into the existing labor insurance program in 1999. The DPP government, which was elected to power in 2000, went even further by introducing a stand-alone unemployment benefits scheme. An unemployment insurance program was legislated in 2003, and expanded unemployment benefits for workers in small firms, including, importantly, income protection for part-time workers (Shi, 2012).

Beginning in the early 2000s, all three governments attempted to reverse some of the regulatory changes that had been made to labor laws a decade earlier. The Taiwan government, for example, passed the Protection Act for Mass Redundancy of Employees in 2003 to stem the growing number of lay-offs. The *re regulation* of the labor laws in Taiwan made it more difficult for employers to lay off large numbers of workers (Shi, 2012). The South Korean government similarly tried to mitigate the effects of labor market precarity when it re-reformed its labor laws, requiring companies to convert part-time and irregular workers with limited term contracts into full-time, standard workers within two years of the start of their employment. Under the new re-regulations, firms were required to formalize their workers so that they benefited from employment security as well as the other social protections that come with full-time work arrangements (Shin, 2010).

The most significant efforts to address labor market flexibility and precariousness for outsiders have been the introduction of *active labor market policies* (ALMPs). According to the OECD, ALMPs include public subsidies to employers, the supply of public sector employment opportunities, resources and programs for vocational training and labor market upskilling, and targeted supports for specific categories of underemployed workers such as young people, women, the elderly, and those who are physically disabled. In addition to unemployment relief, either through income-maintenance schemes (i.e. unemployment benefits for laid-off workers) or efforts to support laid-off workers (i.e. labor market re-regulation), governments in Japan, South Korea, and Taiwan have introduced ALMPs to proactively return unemployed and underemployed workers back into the labor market. The 2003 Employment Insurance program implemented in Taiwan provides, for instance, short-term income relief for laid-off workers as well as vocational training programs to upskill workers. The program provides supports to assist unemployed or underemployed workers to find work. To stimulate the supply side of the labor market, the government has also subsidized the creation of new jobs. In only a few years, the Taiwan government created nearly 10,000 public sector employment opportunities (Shi, 2012).

The South Korea government similarly increased its efforts to stimulate the creation of work opportunities through direct fiscal transfers and subsidies to employers (Yang, 2012). Recently, the government also introduced several new employment support programs for underemployed youths, specifically university and college graduates. It has legislated new childcare programs, which provide state support for young children and frees up women (who are more likely to be involved in child-rearing) to reenter the labor force (Peng and Wong, 2008). Likewise in Japan, the government introduced labor market policies benefiting single mothers, as well as women more generally who are more likely to be employed in nonstandard work. The Japanese government implemented several training and job reentry programs to encourage both younger and elderly workers to enter the labor market. Public funds have also been allocated to incentivize employers to hire youth and elderly workers (Kamimura and Soma, 2013).

Efforts to address labor market dualization have been somewhat effective in mitigating the effects of labor market dualization. Though the share of nonstandard or informal sector workers remains large in Japan and South Korea, the explosive growth in precarious employment leveled off considerably by the 2010s. In Taiwan, the rapid growth in informal and precarious work during the early 2000s flattened during the 2010s.

Yet, despite some success of active labor market policies in creating employment opportunities, the effects of labor market dualization and precariousness for workers remain concerning. Competitive pressures from emerging markets mean that firms in Japan, South Korea, and Taiwan have little choice but to continue to take advantage of flexible employment arrangements, lower wages for nonstandard workers, and fewer social benefits for informally employed workers. In South Korea, there is evidence that firms have dismissed part-time workers before their two-year tenure to avoid converting them to full-time status workers (Shin, 2010). Likewise in Japan, efforts to expand eligibility for unemployment insurance benefits to part-time workers have been offset by the reduction of benefits for laid-off workers (Inaba, 2011). In short, employers have continued to exploit the labor market, despite government efforts to address labor market flexibilization, thus maintaining the precarious status of many workers in post-industrial East Asia.

3.3.2 Targeted Programs

Getting people into or back to work through labor market regulations is one way that governments in Japan, South Korea, and Taiwan have tried to address the challenges of generating employment in the era of post-industrialism. In addition to the introduction of active labor market policies, the East Asian social policy regimes have also implemented policies and measures which seek to mend specific holes in their social safety nets. Segments of the population, described earlier in this section, are especially vulnerable when it comes to employment and social protection in the post-industrial context. Chronic poverty has become a pressing issue in Japan, South Korea, and Taiwan, for instance. Women, elderly workers, and young people continue to be disproportionately excluded from the formal labor market, with little access to the benefits otherwise afforded to formal sector employees. In response, governments have turned to *targeted* social programs that address the challenges faced by specific, vulnerable segments of the population. Ironically, achieving universal social protection has required social policy regimes to take a more targeted approach to address specific groups with specific needs.

Poverty is a growing problem in East Asia. According to a 2004 OECD report, Japan ranked fifth in terms of the number of those living in poverty at 15.3 percent of the population. The poverty rate has largely been concentrated among young people and the elderly. Prevailing stigma around poverty suggests the rate is likely undercounted in Japan, and that the number of those living under the poverty line is actually considerably higher (Tachibanaki, 2006). The government has responded by increasing public assistance benefits that target impoverished households. The distribution of public assistance benefits to households and individuals doubled between 1990 and 2010 (Inaba, 2011: 83). The governments in South Korea and Taiwan have made similar adjustments to their social policy regimes, specifically to increase their targeted public assistance programs.

The rapidly greying societies in Japan, South Korea, and Taiwan reveal another hole in the social safety net. The size and proportion of the elderly population in East Asia have increased dramatically in recent decades According to the World Bank, the proportion of the South Korean population aged 65 years and older was just 3.4 percent in 1960. By 2015, the percentage of the so-called grey population had quadrupled to 13 percent (World Bank). Similarly in Taiwan, the proportion of older people grew from 3.5 percent in 1960 to 12.5 percent in 2015 (Taiwan Statistical Data Book). Over that same period, the proportion of elderly Japanese (65 years and older) increased from 5.6 percent to 26 percent, nearly a fivefold increase. More than one-quarter of Japan's current population is over 65 years old, and South Korea and Taiwan are following this trend (World Bank). Older workers are disproportionately excluded from the labor market. Yet, the elderly require greater access to social protection and programs, such as old-age income security, health care and other social services, including long-term care.

With civil society pressure and advocacy coming from progressive technocrats within the state bureaucracy, the Japanese government introduced a nationwide long-term care (LTC) insurance program in 2000. Japan's LTC scheme is a mandatory program that provides a uniform benefits package for elderly people, including insurance coverage for medical care services. Soon after in 2008, the South Korean government also introduced a publicly subsidized LTC program, modeled after the Japanese scheme (Fleckenstein and Lee, 2017). Enrolment in Korea's long-term care program doubled during the first eight years of the program, proving it to be a needed and popular social benefit. Not surprisingly, Korea's LTC scheme was endorsed by subsequent conservative governments (Jeon and Kwon, 2017). Around the same time, Taiwan announced plans to draft and introduce a similar LTC insurance program. Though the DPP government at the time failed to get the policy implemented, the subsequent KMT-led government introduced a long-term care insurance scheme in 2015, essentially adopting the DPP's original proposal. Targeted social policy benefits for elderly people made political sense for the governments in Japan, South Korea, and Taiwan, winning political support for the incumbent administrations.

Targeted benefits were welcomed because they responded to societal demands and needs, advocated for by civil society groups and issue-based social movements, as well as by state technocrats who viewed such benefits to be complementary to labor market measures. Long-term care benefits proved effective de facto active labor market measures. The provision of long-term care meant that workers who would otherwise exit the labor market to care for elderly family members were able to reenter the labor market. Given patriarchal norms and the expectation that elderly care is the responsibility of the women in the household, the extension of LTC also freed up women to seek employment, thus mitigating some of the negative effects of labor market flexibilization on women described previously (Fleckenstein and Lee, 2017; Peng and Wong, 2008). In other words, social care programs that indirectly incentivized women to return to work were good for those who required care, such as the elderly, and for economic productivity as well. In this respect, long-term care for the elderly appealed to proponents on both the left and right.

In addition to the introduction of LTC programs in East Asia, other social policies targeting women, and specifically mothers, were introduced in Japan, South Korea, and Taiwan during the 2000s. In the absence of robust childcare services, women again are more likely to exit the labor market. The dual burden of work and child-rearing, and of caregiving more generally, leaves single mothers and their children especially vulnerable. Civil society organizations and women's social movements actively campaigned and advocated for the provision of childcare programs. At the same time, government bureaucracies in Japan, South Korea, and Taiwan introduced specialized agencies and ministries dedicated to women and welfare (Peng and Wong, 2008). Together, state and societal advocates pushed for more childcare benefits, targeting specifically working women.

To lower the barriers of entry or reentry into the labor market for women and protect the welfare of children, governments introduced new social policy programs that targeted working mothers and their children. Beginning in the early 2000s, for example, the Taiwan government implemented new labor regulations that extended parental leave (to fathers) and mandated employment security, of which women were the primary beneficiaries. It also introduced measures to increase women's wages, expand childcare facilities, and provide allowances and subsidies for working parents. The South Korean government similarly expanded its infant and childcare programs during the late 1990s and 2000s to target working women and their children. As in Taiwan, the South Korean government invested in publicly funded childcare facilities and provided direct subsidies for childcare at home, as well as for enrolment in public childcare facilities (Peng and Wong, 2008).

3.3.3 Political Accommodation

It is important to point out that in Japan, South Korea, and Taiwan, both progressive and conservative parties pursued targeted social policies as a way to win political support. Neither the so-called progressives nor conservatives could claim to own this social policy reform agenda. As Fleckenstein and Lee observe, "both left and conservative parties, coping with intensified electoral competition, now claim the 'driving seat' in social policy making" (2017: 50). As the examples of Japan, South Korea, and Taiwan demonstrate, in the current post-industrial era, social policies that target precarious workers and especially vulnerable groups are winning platforms, regardless of whether political parties are associated with being more or less progressive. In short, the left and right have *accommodated* social policy reform.

The introduction of active labor market policies (ALMPs) has appealed to voters and been embraced by politicians regardless of their party's ideological position. Active labor market policies were introduced by both progressive and conservative governing parties in Japan, South Korea, and Taiwan because it made political sense for them to do so and because they reinforce both progressive and conservative appeals. For progressives, ALMPs are attractive because they promote greater socioeconomic equity by improving labor market conditions and labor market participation, especially for vulnerable workers such as women and the elderly. For politicians and voters on the right, meanwhile, ALMPs are consistent with their views because they promote employment and work rather than dependence on government subsidies and welfare. The point is that for different reasons and rationales, political actors and voters on the left and right have been able to appeal to active labor market interventions because they facilitate greater equity as well as promote work and labor market participation.

Political proponents on both the left and right have, for different reasons, supported targeted social protection programs aimed at women, their children, and elderly people. Targeted social programs resonate with and appeal to progressives and conservatives. Resources dedicated to subsidizing elderly long-term care and childcare, for instance, are viewed by progressive voters and politicians to be equity-enhancing. They are intended to address the specific inequities faced by precarious workers, notably women. Meanwhile, conservative politicians and employers support targeted social protection schemes because they are effective incentives to motivate and assist workers to return to the labor force, to be economically productive.

In all three cases, accommodation among parties and politicians has helped mitigate and blunt intense political conflict when it comes to social policy reform in the post-industrial era. Active labor market policies and targeted social programs introduced by progressive and conservative governments have endured, and in fact deepened by subsequent administrations. Rarely have governments in Japan, South Korea, and Taiwan undone or dismantled social policy programs that were introduced earlier by their partisan opponents. Rather, successive elected governments, irrespective of whether they are progressive or conservative, have continued to introduce new social programs and social protection initiatives.

Conclusion: Exceptionalism to Universalism

This Element set out to make the case that Japan, South Korea, and Taiwan have achieved a third miracle; that in addition to achieving economic and political miracles – industrialization and democratization – these three societies have thoroughly transformed what were once welfare laggards into more inclusive, robust, government-supported and politically mainstreamed social welfare regimes.

Since the start of the postwar period, over seven decades ago, social spending by East Asian governments has increased; the scope of welfare benefits expanded, and in some cases now universal; and social protection programs have become more expansive to benefit not only formal sector workers, but also increasingly targeting those who are most vulnerable. Regardless of whether the reader is convinced these welfare regimes have approached the "gold standard" welfare state, one has to appreciate the extent to which these East Asian welfare regimes have grown more inclusive and durable over time. Indeed, given global trends since the 1990s, with the onset of globalization and the systematic retrenchment of welfare states worldwide, the social welfare achievements in Japan, South Korea, and Taiwan are all the more remarkable.

This study has also attempted to account for the *distinctive pathway* the East Asian social welfare regimes have taken in their evolution and development, from limited social insurance schemes in the 1950s to more fulsome, if still leaky, social welfare regimes presently. Early social policy reform efforts, I argue in Section 1 of this Element, reflected the postwar developmental states' chief objective at that time, which was to grow their economies. The fulcrum of the Cold War in the region and the imperatives of emerging from out of the Second World War as economic basket cases, Japan, Korea, and Taiwan had little choice but to prioritize growth and productivity. In this context, then, limited social insurance was implemented strategically to placate certain political and economic constituencies, especially during moments of political crisis, but also to bolster economic productivity.

Democratization, I argue in Section 2, reset the rules of the game. Drawing on the example of postwar Japan, where a democratic constitution and political contestation were installed much earlier than in South Korea and Taiwan, the imperative of winning political support (as opposed to quashing dissent) at the ballot box fundamentally altered what governments could and were willing to do when it came to social policy reform. In all three cases, democratic political incentives compelled parties to pursue social policy reform: to universalize social programs, develop new social protection schemes, and to deepen the state's commitment to redistribution.

East Asia's experience with democratic transformation, however, was distinctive, and it affected the course of social welfare reform in the region in distinctive ways. The pathway to deepening democracy and the welfare state in Japan, South Korea, and Taiwan was exceptional. Notably, that the East Asian democracies expanded and universalized parts of their welfare regimes without strong leftist political parties – and indeed, where conservative incumbents led the way in social policy reform – reflects the region's distinctive developmental past (e.g. growth with equity) as well as the unique political context in which democratic parties contest. Contrary to conventional theoretical expectations about the welfare state, ideological flexibility and the ability of East Asian political parties to exploit this open issue space, regardless of their ideological roots and even their autocratic pasts, permitted and incentivized both nominally progressive and conservative parties to deepen their commitments to welfare reform.

To reiterate, the evolution of East Asia's postwar welfare regimes was *exceptional*. The East Asian cases challenge and refine existing theories of how welfare regimes originate and develop. And yet, as discussed in Section 3 of this Element, the region's exceptionalism is giving way to more universal, common challenges faced by *all* advanced economies in the current post-industrial context (see Fleckenstein and Lee, 2017). The recent evolution and future trajectory of East Asia's welfare regimes are converging with those of more established welfare states in the advanced, post-industrial world in two important ways.

First, the consequences of labor market flexibilization and dualization have been similarly experienced in all post-industrial societies. Demographic pressures

Table 2 Public social expenditure (% of GDP)

	2000	2020
USA	14.3	23.9
Canada	15.8	24.9
Germany	25.4	27.9
France	27.5	34.9
UK	17.7	23.9
Japan	16.3	24.9
South Korea	4.5	14.4
Taiwan	8.1	11.9

Sources: https://stats.oecd.org/Index.aspx?
datasetcode=SOCX_AGG; http://ws.dgbas.gov.tw

(i.e. lower birth rates) felt across all post-industrial societies have also similarly increased the stresses on labor markets and welfare states, as well as fomented intense political debates about immigration policy and the extension of social safety nets to migrants. East Asia's deepening commitment to social protection, reflected in the growth in social spending in recent years, is not unique; rather, it is on-trend with other post-industrial societies. Public spending on social welfare (see Table 2) has increased significantly in other advanced post-industrial economies. Importantly, however, most of the growth in spending is accounted for by new targeted social policy initiatives that are similar to the ones that have emerged in East Asia, specifically in housing, poverty alleviation and public assistance, unemployment, and active labor market policies programs.

Second, as argued in this Element, the pressures associated with post-industrialism, notably the flexibilization and dualization of labor markets, have revealed new sources of precarity and vulnerability in East Asia and elsewhere. These post-industrial pressures have required new forms of targeted social protection. The growth in nonstandard informal sector work portends the "old model" of welfare statism, which centered on the interests of organized formal sectors workers, needs to start accommodating a new array of socioeconomic winners and losers. Increased social spending on active labor market policies, public assistance, and unemployment marks a significant departure from more traditional concerns of the welfare state. Universalism has ceded to more targeted social policy interventions, including labor market policies and interventions aimed at specific segments of the population. In other words, contemporary welfare regimes, in East Asia and elsewhere, have evolved from a commitment to universal safety nets to many targeted safety nets. The ways in which East Asia's welfare regimes have responded to current social and economic pressures are less and less exceptional.

To conclude, the challenges faced by social policymakers and progressive social policy advocates in Japan, South Korea, and Taiwan are increasingly similar to other regions. Simply put, *East Asia's welfare state challenges are universal welfare state challenges*. New and innovative theories of the post-industrial welfare state are required, and to that end, East Asian cases need to be included in these comparative conversations, to not only shed new empirical light on the evolution of post-industrial welfare states, but to also contribute to the development of new theoretical insights into how social welfare regimes must adapt to current political economic realities.

References

Amsden, Alice. *Asia's Next Giant: South Korea and Late Industrialization.* Oxford University Press, 1989.

Asian Development Bank. *Key Indicators of Asian and Pacific Countries.* 2020.

Breznitz, Dan. *Innovation and the State: Political Choice and Strategies for Growth in Israel, Taiwan and Ireland.* Yale University Press, 2007.

Calder, Kent. *Crisis and Compensation: Public Policy and Political Stability in Japan.* Princeton University Press, 1988.

Campbell, John and Naoki Ikegami. *The Art of Balance in Health Policy: Maintaining Japan's Low-Cost Egalitarian System.* Cambridge University Press, 1998.

Chan, Kam Wah. "Deconstructing the Asian Welfare Model: Social Equality Matters." *Journal of Asian Public Policy* (Vol. 1, No. 3, 2008).

Chao, Linda and Ramon Myers. *The First Chinese Democracy: Political Life in the Republic of China on Taiwan.* Johns Hopkins University Press, 1998.

Cheng, Tun-Jen. "Political Regimes and Development Strategies: South Korea and Taiwan," in Gary Gereffi and Donald Wyman, eds., *Manufacturing Miracles: Paths of Industrialization in Latin America and East Asia.* Princeton University Press, 1990.

Chi, Eunju and Hyeok Long Kwon. "Unequal New Democracies in East Asia: Rising Inequality and Government Responses in South Korea and Taiwan." *Asian Survey* (Vol. 52, No. 5, 2012).

Cho, Sungik and Yool Choi. "Convergent or Divergent? The Hidden Dynamics of Institutional Changes in the Labor Markets and Social Welfare Systems in South Korea and Japan." *Politics and Policy* (Vol. 45, No. 4, 2017).

Chu, Yin-Wah. "Labor and Democratization in South Korea and Taiwan." *Journal of Contemporary Asia* (Vol. 28, No. 2, January, 1998).Cotton, James. "From Authoritarianism to Democracy in South Korea." *Political Studies* (Vol. 37, No. 2, 1989).

Deyo, Frederic. *Beneath the Miracle: Labor Subordination in the New Asian Industrialism.* University of California Press, 1989.

Deyo, Frederic, Stephan Haggard, and Hagen Koo. "Labor in the Political Economy of East Asian Industrialization." *Bulletin of Concerned Asian Scholars* (Vol. 19, No. 2, 1987).

Dower, John. *Embracing Defeat: Japan in the Wake of World War II.* W.W. Norton, 1999.

Emmenegger, Patrick, Silja Hausermann, Bruno Palier, and Martin Seeleib-Kaiser, eds. *The Age of Dualization: The Changing Face of Inequality in Deindustrializing Societies*. Oxford University Press, 2012.

Esping-Andersen, Gosta. *Three Worlds of Welfare Capitalism*. Princeton University Press, 1990.

Estevez-Abe, Margarita. *Welfare and Capitalism in Postwar Japan*. Cambridge University Press, 2008.

Estevez-Abe, Margarita, Torben Iverson, and David Soskice. "Social Protection and the Formation of Skills: A Reinterpretation of the Welfare State," in Peter Hall and David Soskice, eds., *Varieties of Capitalism*. Oxford University Press, 2001.

Evans, Peter. *Embedded Autonomy: States and Industrial Transformation*. Princeton University Press, 1995.

Fleckenstein, Timo and Soohyun Christine Lee. "Democratization, Post-Industrialization, and East Asian Welfare Capitalism: The Politics of Welfare State Reform in Japan, South Korea and Taiwan." *Journal of International and Comparative Social Policy* (Vol. 33, No. 1, 2017).

Garay, Candelaria. *Social Policy Expansion in Latin America*. Cambridge University Press, 2017.

Goodman, Roger, Gordon White, and Huck-Ju Kwon, eds. *The East Asian Welfare Model: Welfare Orientalism and the State*. Routledge, 1998.

Goodman, Roger and Ito Peng. "The East Asian Welfare States: Peripatetic Learning, Adaptive Change and Nation-Building," in Gosta Esping-Andersen, ed., *Welfare States in Transition: National Adaptations in Global Economies*. Sage, 1996.

Gottfried, Heidi. "Precarious Work in Japan: Old Forms, New Risks." *Journal of Contemporary Asia* (Vol. 44, No. 3, 2014).

Gough, Ian and Geof Wood, eds. *Insecurity and Welfare Regimes in Asia, Africa and Latin America*. Cambridge University Press, 2004.

Haggard, Stephan. *Pathways from the Periphery: The Politics of Growth in the Newly Industrializing Countries*. Cornell University Press, 1990.

Haggard, Stephan and Robert Kaufman. *Development, Democracy and Welfare States: Latin America, East Asia and Eastern Europe*. Princeton University Press, 2009.

Haggard, Stephan and Robert Kaufman. *The Political Economy of Democratic Transitions*. Princeton University Press, 1995.

Hatch, Walter. *Asia's Flying Geese: How Regionalization Shapes Japan*. Cornell University Press, 2011.

Holliday, Ian. "East Asian Social Policy in the Wake of the Financial Crisis: Farewell to Productivism?" *Policy and Politics* (Vol. 33, No. 1, 2005).

Holliday, Ian. "Productivist Welfare Capitalism: Social Policy in East Asia." *Political Studies* (Vol. 48, No. 4, 2000).

Hsiao, Michael, ed. *East Asian Middle Classes in Comparative Perspective.* Institute of Ethnology, 1999.

Hsiao, Michael Hsin-Huang. "Precarious Work in Taiwan: A Profile." *American Behavioral Scientist* (Vol. 57, No. 3, 2013).

Huntington, Samuel. *The Third Wave: Democratization in the Late Twentieth Century.* University of Oklahoma Press, 1991.

Hwang, Gyu-Jin. "Explaining Welfare State Adaptation in East Asia: The Cases of Japan, Korea and Taiwan." *Asian Journal of Social Science* (Vol. 40, No. 2, 2012).

Ide, Eisaku. "The Rise and Fall of the Industrious State: Why Did Japan's Welfare State Differ from European-Style Models?" in Gisela Huerlimann, W. Elliot Brownlee, and Eisaku Ide, eds., *Worlds of Taxation*. Palgrave, 2018.

Imada, Takatoshi. "The Japanese Middle Class and Politics after World War II," in Michael Hsiao, ed., *East Asian Middle Classes in Comparative Perspective*. Institute of Ethnology, Academia Sinica, 1999.

Immergut, Ellen. *Health Politics: Interests and Institutions in Western Europe.* Cambridge University Press, 1992.

Inaba, Miyuki. "Increasing Poverty in Japan: Social Policy and Public Assistance Program." *Asian Social Work and Policy Review* (Vol. 5, 2011).

Jeon, Boyoung and Soonman Kwon. "Health and Long-Term Care Systems for Older People in the Republic of Korea: Policy Challenges and Lessons." *Health Systems Reform* (Vol. 3, No. 3, 2017).

Johnson, Chalmers. "The Developmental State: Odyssey of a Concept," in Meredith Woo-Cumings, ed., *The Developmental State*. Cornell University Press, 1999.

Johnson, Chalmers. *MITI and the Japanese Miracle: The Growth of Industrial Policy, 1925–1975*. Stanford University Press, 1982.

Jones, Catherine. "Hong Kong, Singapore, South Korea and Taiwan: Oikonomic Welfare States." Government and Opposition (Vol. 25, No. 4, 1990).

Jones, Catherine. "The Pacific Challenge: Confucian Welfare States," in Catherine Jones, ed., *New Perspectives on the Welfare State in Europe*. Routledge, 1993.

Kamimura, Yasuhiro and Naoko Soma. "Active Labor Market Policies in Japan: A Shift Away from the Company-Centered Model?" *Journal of Asian Public Policy* (Vol. 6, No. 1, 2013).

Kasza, Gregory. "The Rise (and Fall?) of Social Equality: The Evolution of Japan's Welfare State," in Alisa Gaunder, ed., *Routledge Handbook of Japanese Politics*. Routledge, 2011.

Kasza, Gregory. "War and Welfare in Japan." *The Journal of Asian Studies* (Vol. 61, No. 2, 2002).

Kezier, Arjan. "Non-regular Employment in Japan: Continued and Renewed Dualities." *Work, Employment and Society* (Vol. 22, No. 3, 2008).

Kim, Hak-Jae. "Three Dualization Processes in Korea: The Labor Market, Welfare Policy and Political Representation." *Development and Society* (Vol. 45, No. 2, 2016).

Kim, Hyun-Young. "From a Dualized Labor Market to a Dualized Welfare State: Employment Insecurity and Welfare State Development in South Korea." *International Area Studies Review* (Vol. 20, No. 1, 2017).

Kim, Jun Il and Jongryn Mo. "Democratization and Macroeconomic Policy," in Chung-In Moon and Jongryn Mo, eds., *Democracy and the Korean Economy.* Hoover Institution Press, 1999.

Korpi, Walter. *The Democratic Class Struggle*. Routledge, 1983.

Ku, Ycun-Wen. *Welfare Capitalism in Taiwan: State, Economy and Social Policy.* MacMillan, 1997.

Kume, Ikuo. *Disparaged Success: Labor Politics in Postwar Japan.* Cornell University Press, 1998.

Kume, Ikuo. *Disparaged Success: Labor Politics in Postwar Japan.* Cornell University Press, 2004.

Kwon, Huck-Ju. "Transforming the Developmental Welfare State in East Asia." UNRISD, *Social Policy and Development Program Paper*, No. 22, 2005.

Kwon, Huck-Ju. "Democracy and the Politics of Social Welfare: A comparative Analysis of Welfare Systems in East Asia," in Roger Goodman, Gordon White and Huck-Ju Kwon, eds., *The East Asian Welfare Model: Welfare Orientalism and the State.* Routledge, 1998.

Kwon, Huck-Ju. *The Welfare State in Korea: The Politics of Legitimation.* St. Martin's Press, 1999.

Kwon, Soonman. "Future of Long-Term Care Financing for the Elderly in Korea." *Aging Social Policy* (Vol. 20, No. 1, 2008).

Lee, Namhee. *The Making of Minjung: Democracy and the Politics of Representation in South Korea*. Cornell University Press, 2007.

Lee, Sang-Chul and Karlyn Campbell. "Korean President Roh Tae-Woo's 1988 Inaugural Address: Campaigning for Investiture." *Quarterly Journal of Speech* (Vol. 80, No. 1, 1994).

Lee, Sophia Seung-Yoon. "Institutional Legacy of State Corporatism in De-industrial Labor Markets: A Comparative Study of Japan, South Korea and Taiwan." *Socio-Economic Review* (Vol. 14, No. 1, 2016).

Lee, Sophia Seung-Yoon. "The Shift of Labor Market Risks in Deindustrializing Taiwan, Japan and Korea." *Perspectives on Global Development and Technology* (Vol. 10, No. 2, 2011).

Lee, Yoonkyun. "Varieties of Labor Politics in Northeast Asian Democracies: Political Institutions and Union Activism in Korea and Taiwan." *Asian Survey* (Vol. 46, No. 5, 2006).

Lee, Yeonho and Sukkyu Chung. "Labor and Politics in East Asia: The Case of Failure of Encompassing Labor Organizations in Korea." *Asia Perspective* (Vol. 32, No. 3, 2008).

Lin, Chenwei. "Weak Taxation and Constraints of the Welfare State in Democratized Taiwan." *Japanese Journal of Political Science* (Vol. 19, 2018).

Lin, Wan-I and Wen-Chi Grace Chou. "Globalization, Regime Transformation and Social Policy Development in Taiwan," in James Lee and Kam Wah Chan, eds., *The Crisis of Welfare in East Asia*. Lexington Books, 2007.

Lindert, Peter. *Growing Public: Social Spending and Economic Growth since the 18th Century.* Cambridge University Press, 2004.

Looney, Kristen. *Mobilizing for Development: The Modernization of Rural East Asia*. Cornell University Press, 2020.

Milly, Deborah. *Poverty, Equality and Growth: The Politics of Need in Postwar Japan*. Harvard University Press, 1999.

Miura, Mari. *Welfare through Work: Conservative Ideas, Partisan Dynamics and Social Protection in Japan*. Cornell University Press, 2012.

Moody, Peter. *Political Change on Taiwan: A Study of Ruling Party Adaptability*. Praeger, 1992.

Moon, Chung-in. "Democratization and Globalization as Ideological and Political Foundations of Economic Policy," in Chung-In Moon and Jongryn Mo, eds., *Democracy and the Korean Economy*. Hoover Institution Press, 1999.

Pempel, T. J., ed. *The Politics of the Asian Economic Crisis*. Cornell University Press, 1999.

Pempel, T. J. and Keiichi Tsunekawa. "Corporatism without Labor? The Japanese Anomaly," in Philippe Schmitter and Gerhard Lehmbruch, eds., *Trends towards Corporatist Intermediation*. Sage, 1979.

Peng, Ito. "Labor Market Dualization in Japan and South Korea," in Patrick Emmenegger, Silja Häusermann, Bruno Palier, and Martin Seeleib-Kaiser, eds., *The Age of Dualization: The Changing Face of Inequality in Deindustrializing Societies*. Oxford University Press, 2012.

Peng, Ito. "Postindustrial Pressures, Political Regimes Shifts and Social Policy Reform in Japan and South Korea." *Journal of East Asian Studies* (Vol. 4, No. 3, 2004).

Peng, Ito and Joseph Wong. "East Asia," in Frances Castles, Stephan Leibfried, Jane Lewis, Herbert Obinger, and Christopher Pierson, eds., *Oxford Handbook of the Welfare State*. Oxford University Press, 2010.

Peng, Ito and Joseph Wong. "Institutions and Institutional Purpose: Continuity and Change in East Asian Social Policy." *Politics and Society* (Vol. 36, No. 1, 2008), 61–88.

Pye, Lucian. *Asian Power and Politics: The Cultural Dimensions of Authority.* Harvard University Press, 1985.

Ramesh, M. *Social Policy in East and Southeast Asia: Education, Health, Housing and Income Maintenance*. Routledge, 2004.

Ringen, Stein. *The Korean State and Social Policy: How Korea Lifted Itself from Poverty and Dictatorship to Affluence and Democracy.* Oxford University Press, 2011.

Rueda, David. *Social Democracy Inside-Out: Partisanship and Labor Market Policy in Advanced Industrialized Democracies*. Oxford University Press, 2008.

Shi, Shih-Jiunn. "Shifting Dynamics of Welfare Politics in Taiwan: From Income Maintenance to Labor Protection." *Journal of Asian Public Policy* (Vol. 5, No. 1, 2012).

Shim, Jaemin. "Left Is Right and Right Is Left? Partisan Difference on Social Welfare and Particularistic Benefits in Japan, South Korea and Taiwan." *Journal of International and Comparative Social Policy* (Vol. 36, No. 1, 2020).

Shim, Jaemin. "The Legislature and Agenda Politics of Social Welfare: A Comparative Analysis of Authoritarian and Democratic Regimes in South Korea." *Democratization* (Vol. 26, No. 7, 2019).

Shin, Doh-Chull and Richard Rose. "Responding to Economic Crisis: The 1998 New Korea Barometer Survey." *Studies in Public Policy* 311 (Center for the Study of Public Policy, University of Strathclyde, 1998).

Shin, Kwang-Yeong. "Globalization and Social Inequality in South Korea," in Jesook Song, ed., *New Millennium in South Korea: Neoliberal Capitalism and Transnational Movements*. Routledge, 2010.

Shizume, Masato, Masatoshi Kato, and Ryozo Matsuda. "A Corporate-Centered Conservative Welfare Regime: Three Layered Protection in Japan." *Journal of Asian Public Policy* (Vol. 14, No. 1, 2021).

Skocpol, Theda. *Protecting Soldiers and Mothers: The Political Origins of Social Policy in the United States.* Harvard University Press, 1995.

Slater, Dan and Joseph Wong. *From Development to Democracy: The Transformations of Modern Asia*. Princeton University Press, 2022.

Slater, Dan and Joseph Wong. "The Strength to Concede: Ruling Parties and Democratization in Developmental Asia." *Perspectives on Politics* (Vol. 11, No. 3, 2013).

Solt, Frederick. "The Standardized World Income Inequality Database Version 8–9, Harvard Dataverse." 2019. https://dataverse.harvard.edu/dataset.xhtml?persistentId=doi:10.7910/DVN/LM4OWF.

Son, Annette Hye Kyung. "Social Insurance Programs in South Korea and Taiwan: A Historical Overview." *Uppsala Papers in Economic History*, Report No. 50, 2002.

Son, Annette Hye Kyung. "Taiwan's Path to National Health Insurance (1950–1995)." *International Journal of Social Welfare* (Vol. 10, No. 1, 2001).

Song, Ho Keun. "The Birth of the Welfare State in Korea: The Unfinished Symphony of Democratization and Globalization." *Journal of East Asian Studies* (Vol. 3, No. 3, 2003).

Song, Ho Keun. *Labour Unions in the Republic of Korea: Challenge and Choice*. International Institute for Labour Studies, 1999.

Stephens, John D. *Transition from Capitalism to Socialism*. Macmillan, 1979.

Tachibanaki, Toshiaki. "Inequality and Poverty in Japan." *The Japanese Economic Review* (Vol. 57, No. 1, 2006).

Tanaka, Takuji. "Japanese Welfare State in Comparative Perspective: An Overview." *Hitotsubashai Bulletin of Social Sciences* (Vol. 11, 2019).

Wade, Robert. *Governing the Market: Economic Theory and the Role of Government in East Asian Industrialization*. Princeton University Press, 1990.

Watanabe, Hiroaki Richard. "Labor Market Dualism and Diversification in Japan." *British Journal of Industrial Relations* (Vol. 56, No. 3, 2018).

Watkins, Kevin. *Economic Growth with Equity: Lessons from East Asia*. Oxfam, 1998.

White, Gordon and Roger Goodman. "Welfare Orientalism and the Search for an East Asian Welfare Model," in Roger Goodman, Huck-Ju Kwon, and Gordon White, eds., *The East Asian Welfare Model: Welfare Orientalism and the State*. Routledge, 1998.

Wilensky, Harold. *The Welfare State and Equality*. University of California Press, 1967.

Wong, Joseph. "Healthy Democracies and Welfare Politics in Taiwan: The Arguments, Refinements and Limitations," in Dafydd Fell and Michael Hsiao, eds., *Taiwan Studies Revisited*. Routledge Press, 2019.

Wong, Joseph. "East Asian Democratization and the Welfare State," in Tun-Jen Cheng and Yun-Han Chu, eds., *Handbook on East Asian Democratization*. Routledge, 2018.

Wong, Joseph. "Adapting to Democracy: Societal Mobilization and Social Policy in Taiwan and South Korea." *Studies in Comparative International Development* (Vol. 40, No. 3, 2005).

Wong, Joseph. *Healthy Democracies: Welfare Politics in Taiwan and South Korea*. Cornell University Press, 2004a.

Wong, Joseph. "Democratization and the Left: Comparing East Asia and Latin America." *Comparative Political Studies* (Vol. 37, No. 10, 2004b).

Wong, Joseph. "Resisting Reform: The Politics of Health Care in Democratizing Taiwan." *American Asian Review: An International Journal of Modern and Contemporary Asia* (Vol. 21, No. 2, 2003).

Wong, Joseph. *Betting on Biotech: Innovation and the Limits of Asia's Developmental State*. Cornell University Press, 2011.

Woo, Jung-Eun. *Race to the Swift: State and Finance in Korean Industrialization*. Columbia University Press, 1991.

World Bank. *The East Asian Miracle: Economic Growth and Public Policy*. Oxford University Press, 1993.

Yang, Jae-Jin. "Parochial Welfare Politics and the Small Welfare State in South Korea." *Comparative Politics* (Vol. 45, No. 4, 2019).

Yang, Jae-Jin. "The Korean Welfare State in Economic Hard Times: Democracy, Partisanship and Social Learning." *Taiwan Journal of Democracy* (Vol. 8, No. 1, 2012).

Yang, Jae-Jin. "Parochial Welfare Politics and the Small Welfare State in South Korea." *Comparative Politics* (Vol. 45, No. 4, 2013).

You, Jong-Il. "Income Distribution and Growth in East Asia." *Journal of Development Studies* (Vol. 34, No. 6, 1998).

www.ingramcontent.com/pod-product-compliance
Ingram Content Group UK Ltd.
Pitfield, Milton Keynes, MK11 3LW, UK
UKHW022023010225
454381UK00030B/757